FROM PAYCHECK TO FREEDOM

WHY OWNING A BUSINESS IS THE FASTEST AND EASIEST PATH TO FINANCIAL PROSPERITY

FROM PAYCHECK TO FREEDOM

WHY OWNING A BUSINESS IS THE FASTEST AND EASIEST PATH TO FINANCIAL PROSPERITY

TOM WHEELWRIGHT, CPA
BEAU ECKSTEIN

ethos
collective

Printed in the United States of America

Published by Igniting Souls
PO Box 43, Powell, OH 43065
IgnitingSouls.com

LCCN: 2024945703
Paperback ISBN: 978-1-63680-374-6
Hardcover ISBN: 978-1-63680-375-3
e-book ISBN: 978-1-63680-376-0

Available in paperback, hardcover, e-book, and audiobook.

Dedication

To all the mentors who have guided me, inspired me, and challenged me to grow—I am forever grateful. Your wisdom and generosity have shaped not only this book but also the person I am today.

To the thousands of entrepreneurs I've had the privilege of meeting along this journey, thank you for sharing your stories and dreams. You are the reason I continue to push forward. Each of you has fueled the fire in my belly that drives me to do more, be more, and give more.

This book is for all of you.

—Beau Eckstein

Table of Contents

Foreword
by Robert Kiyosaki

In 1974, I completed my six-year contract with the US Marine Corps, which was in exchange for flight training. I flew helicopter gunships in Vietnam. As a Marine Corps officer, I wanted to fight from the air rather than on foot in the jungles.

My flight training was impeccable. Flight school came in two phases. Beginning and then advanced.

Although I crashed three times in Vietnam, I am alive today because, in advanced pilot training, I had great instructor pilots. These pilots had just returned from Vietnam and taught new pilots from real-world combat experience.

If I had gone to fly in Vietnam without instruction from pilots with actual combat experience, I am certain I would not have returned home alive.

As you know, our schools are filled with teachers who lack real-world experience. Most academics entered school at the age of five and never left. They live in their own fantasy worlds, unable to prepare students for the real world.

When I returned from Vietnam, my poor dad suggested I fly with the airline. My problem was I wanted to become an entrepreneur like my rich dad. I did not want to be an employee like my poor dad.

At first, I considered buying a franchise. I looked at several. A hamburger franchise, a pizza franchise, and a used car franchise, to name a few. I also went to the Better Business Bureau to look for established businesses for sale.

The problem was that I did not have much money and decided that a franchise was too expensive. Worst of all, I lacked real-world business experience.

So, like many entrepreneurs who dream of being the next Steve Jobs, Bill Gates, or Elon Musk, I decided to just "Go for it."

In 1974, I started the first nylon and Velcro surfer wallet business. Although I achieved considerable success, the price of that success was very high. It was a price paid in pain: pain from betrayal, corruption, and massive money losses.

My rich dad had refused to invest in my "start-up" because he did not trust my two "partners." My rich dad's instincts were correct. My two partners turned out to be con-men and cowards. When the going got tough, they took off with money... the money I raised from investors—investors like my poor dad.

It took me over twelve long years to finally repay all my investors.

In retrospect, the pizza franchise I almost bought would have been a bargain.

Today, I am often asked whether people should start their own business or purchase a franchise.

A new entrepreneur should seriously consider a franchise, not for the pizza dough recipe but for the education, operating guidelines, and wisdom, which can be priceless. Obviously, the quality of the franchisor makes a difference.

Simply said, becoming an entrepreneur is not an easy process, and success depends upon the quality of the people involved in the entrepreneur's process.

As my rich dad often said:

"Business is easy. Finding good people to do business with is hard."

I have worked with Tom Wheelwright for over twenty-five years. He is my accountant, but more importantly, my teacher. Much like the instructor pilots who prepared me for Vietnam, Tom has kept me alive in the treacherous world of business. Most importantly, Tom has guided me when dealing with bureaucrats, especially the tax collectors.

When I need real-world guidance or simply someone to lean on, I call on Tom Wheelwright. He is an excellent CPA, business owner, and friend.

Speaking of friends, I have written two books with now President Donald Trump. I got to know him and his family well. Donald Trump's two sons, Don Jr. and Eric Trump, and I spent a lot of time hunting.

Over the years working with "The Donald," before being introduced to someone he did not know, he often asked: "Are they good people?"

Whether you create your own "start-up" from scratch, buy an existing one, or purchase a franchise, may you have the good fortune of meeting and doing business with "good people."

Doing business and learning from honest, competent, good people, like Tom Wheelwright, are some of my greatest joys in life.

I would have never experienced such joy if I had followed my poor dad's advice: Poor dad's advice was to get a job, fly for the airlines, and get my PhD just for added "job security."

More than money, my poor dad valued job security, a steady paycheck, and great benefits, such as a 401(k) retirement plan, two weeks of paid vacation a year, and a promotion ladder to climb.

I am glad I did not follow my poor dad's advice. If I had, I would never have experienced the ups and downs, highs and lows, of doing business in the real world.

Learning to do business as an entrepreneur rather than an employee has not been easy. Yet, it has allowed me to meet many interesting, successful, real-world business people like Tom Wheelwright and President Donald Trump.

Best of luck.

Foreword by Robert Kiyosaki
Author of *Rich Dad Poor Dad*
The #1 Personal Finance Book of All Time

A Note to the Reader

Welcome to an exciting journey that goes far beyond just starting a business. This is about discovering what's possible when you embrace your potential and align it with your goals, values, and vision for the future. The pages ahead aren't just about financial know-how—they're about growth, resilience, and creating a life of purpose and impact. This book is more than a resource; it's a guide to transforming your ambitions into action.

From Paycheck to Freedom – Why Owning a Business is the Fastest and Easiest Way to Financial Prosperity was written with the understanding that every business decision is deeply personal. Beneath each choice is a truth waiting to be uncovered—about what drives you, what matters most, and what you're capable of achieving. As a Performance Enhancement Coach, I've always believed that the answers we're looking for are already within us. It's not about chasing new wisdom—it's about uncovering the incredible insights you already have. This book is here to help you uncover those insights and trust your instincts as you navigate the world of business ownership.

Many of us hold back when it comes to success—not because we doubt our ability, but because the idea of achieving our full potential can be intimidating. It's easier to stay in our comfort zones than to face the responsibilities that come with success. But this book challenges you to step up. It's not just about achieving business goals; it's about fulfilling your own personal destiny.

Each chapter offers practical tools and strategies to help you move forward with confidence—whether it's understanding SBA loans, exploring funding options, or creating a business plan that speaks to your vision. These are more than just steps to build a business; they're opportunities to create something that reflects who you are and what you stand for.

As you explore these topics, remember that every financial decision, every plan, and every risk is a step toward building not just a business but a life of purpose and fulfillment. The process of entrepreneurship isn't just about spreadsheets and strategies—it's about creating something meaningful that aligns with your values.

I encourage you to approach this journey with an open mind and a courageous heart. Use the insights in this book as tools to stretch beyond what you thought was possible. Let it serve as both a mirror reflecting your aspirations and a map guiding you toward them.

—Beau Eckstein

1

The Entrepreneurial Dream Redefined

The path from paycheck to freedom is a journey from the known to the vast expanse of the unknown. For many, being a W2 employee offers a semblance of security—a steady income, predictable hours, and the comfort of routine. Yet, beneath this surface of stability lies a current of desire for more: more control, more freedom, and, ultimately, more fulfillment. This is where the entrepreneurial dream begins.

Entrepreneurship represents not just a career choice but a shift in lifestyle and mindset. It is a declaration of independence from the traditional employment model and a step toward the reimagined American Dream—a dream where financial freedom and personal achievement are not just aspirational but attainable. This journey offers challenges and uncertainties. Yet, for those up to the task, the confrontation of these obstacles will kindle the allure and true spirit of entrepreneurship. These pioneers will discover rewards that extend far beyond financial gain, touching the very core of what it means to be autonomous, creative, and, ultimately, empowered.

The Viable Alternative to the Nine-to-Five

For generations, the W2 arrangement has been the default path. This model offers a certain level of security and predictability. Employees can enjoy set hours and regular paychecks. Many employers offer benefits such as health insurance and retirement plans. Few understand the price of this security: limited potential for growth, dependence on the employer's success, and minimal control over one's career trajectory.

Against this backdrop, entrepreneurship is a compelling alternative for those seeking more from their professional lives. Entrepreneurs have the unique opportunity to be their own boss, make their own decisions, and shape the direction of their business. Most entrepreneurs cite this level of autonomy and control as one of the most gratifying aspects of business ownership.

Some downplay the viability of business ownership because of the financial risks, responsibility, pressure, and emotional toll entrepreneurship puts on the individual. Yes, you'll need some starting capital, and there's always the risk your business may not succeed. Financial uncertainty is part of entrepreneurial life, especially in the early stages. Entrepreneurs must be decisive, resilient, and determined. Plus, it takes discipline to balance the long hours of a growing business and the demands of your personal life. The highs and lows of entrepreneurship can take an emotional toll, and many entrepreneurs have to navigate the learning curve as they turn their passion into expertise or make their expertise an actual business.

The journey from W2 employee to entrepreneur is a transformative process that involves significant changes in lifestyle and professional focus. This transition can be both exhilarating and daunting. It necessitates leaving behind the familiar structures of traditional employment for the dynamic and often unpredictable world of owning a business.

Though these endeavors involve risk and uncertainty, they also offer tremendous potential. First, you have multiple customers. As a W2 employee, you have only one customer: your boss. If you lose this client, it means you lose your job. As a business owner, you diversify. One disgruntled customer will not mean you lose your entire business.

Businesses that scale successfully give their owners significantly higher earnings than one can make in most traditional employment settings. Additionally, satisfaction and fulfillment levels rise when individuals pursue their passions and build businesses around what they genuinely care about.

While the hours for business owners can be long, they can also be very flexible. And entrepreneurs get to choose their work environment and business model. Whether it's a brick-and-mortar store, an online business, a franchise, or a business-to-business (B2B) service provider, their chosen model can help increase their sense of purpose as they create jobs, innovate, and contribute to their communities and economies. This ability to make a tangible difference becomes a powerful motivator.

Understanding the benefits and challenges of entrepreneurship is crucial for anyone considering this path. It requires a specific blend of passion, resilience, and strategic planning. By embracing the entrepreneurial spirit, individuals open themselves to a world of possibilities where they can forge their own paths, create value, and achieve a sense of fulfillment that transcends financial success.

Securing the knowledge and skills necessary to run your business is a big part of the transformation. From product development and marketing to sales and financial planning, a first-time business owner needs a firm handle on how much personal savings they need, the cost of starting a business, how to get their product to market, and the possibility of fluctuating income.

Much of this knowledge can be attained through building a support network. Mentors, peers, and advisors can offer guidance, support, and feedback. This network can provide emotional support, practical advice, and connections to help navigate the challenges of starting and growing a business. Additionally, these seasoned entrepreneurs will be able to give you advice and send you in the right direction to maneuver through the legal and administrative requirements, such as registering the business, understanding tax implications, and complying with relevant regulations. Getting these aspects right from the start is crucial for the long-term success and legitimacy of the company.

Understanding the Allure of Entrepreneurship

Entrepreneurship is undeniably alluring for many, promising a path to financial success, personal fulfillment, and independence. At its core, the draw of entrepreneurship can be attributed to several key desires that resonate with individuals from various backgrounds and walks of life.

One of the fundamental motivations driving people into the entrepreneurial journey is the desire for autonomy. The prospect of being one's own boss, making decisions that directly impact the business's success, and steering its direction offers a sense of control most don't find in traditional employment.

Sara Blakely, the founder of Spanx, embodies the entrepreneurial pursuit of autonomy. Starting with a simple idea to improve women's undergarments, Blakely navigated the entrepreneurial world without formal training in fashion or business. Her determination to retain control over her product and vision led to Spanx becoming a billion-dollar company, with Blakely maintaining a significant stake in the business she built from scratch.

Other entrepreneurs find motivation in the opportunity to turn their passion or dream into a viable business. Not only do they want to make a living, but they also want to build a life aligned with their values, interests, and passions. Entrepreneurship offers them a unique platform to create products, services, or solutions that reflect their personal vision and build a business around what they truly care about.

Yvon Chouinard, founder of Patagonia, turned his passion for rock climbing and the outdoors into an iconic brand that promotes environmental activism and sustainable practices. Chouinard's journey from a self-taught blacksmith making climbing gear to leading a global company demonstrates how a personal passion can evolve into a business that impacts the world.

While entrepreneurship involves financial risk, it also offers the potential for significant financial reward. The possibility of achieving financial independence, with the freedom to live life on one's own terms, is a powerful motivator.

Jeff Bezos, the founder of Amazon, left a comfortable job in finance to start an online bookstore from his garage. His vision extended far beyond selling books. He wanted to build a customer-centric company that could sell everything online.

Amazon's monumental growth transformed Bezos into one of the world's wealthiest individuals, illustrating the unparalleled financial potential of successful entrepreneurship.

The journeys of Sara Blakely, Yvon Chouinard, and Jeff Bezos highlight the diversity of entrepreneurial paths. From retail and fashion to outdoor gear and global e-commerce, these stories show that entrepreneurship can thrive in various industries. Each story is unique, reflecting different motivations, challenges, and outcomes. Yet, they all share common themes of autonomy, passion, and the pursuit of financial independence. The success stories of entrepreneurs across different fields serve as both inspiration and proof that with passion, resilience, and a willingness to embrace risk, it's possible to transform a vision into reality.

What Kind of Entrepreneur Will You Be?

Success stories that illustrate the diversity of paths to entrepreneurship and the various motivations behind them dot the entrepreneurial landscape. As you think about how you might move from paycheck to freedom, let's look at some areas with high potential.

1. **The Tech Innovator:** One software developer worked in the tech industry for many years before he decided to launch a startup that revolutionized how businesses interact with their customers online. Driven by a passion for technology and a desire to solve complex problems, this entrepreneur's journey from employee to founder of a multimillion-dollar company underscores the potential of turning technical expertise into a successful business venture.

2. **The Creative Entrepreneur:** We can also consider a freelance graphic designer who turned her work into a full-fledged branding agency. Her desire for creative freedom and autonomy led her to find a space to pursue projects aligned with her artistic vision and values. Today, her agency helps startups and established businesses create impactful brand identities, showcasing how a passion for creativity can be the foundation of a thriving business.

3. **The Social Innovator:** Another inspiring example comes from a former non-profit worker who founded a social enterprise focused on sustainable agriculture. Motivated by a desire to make a positive impact on the environment and communities, this entrepreneur's path highlights how business can be a force for social good. Through innovative farming techniques and community programs, the enterprise not only turns a profit but also contributes to societal change.

4. **The Lifestyle Entrepreneur:** Consider the story of an individual who left a high-stress corporate job to start a wellness retreat in a tropical paradise. Seeking a healthier work-life balance and the opportunity to promote wellness and mindfulness, this entrepreneur's venture offers clients a chance to escape the hustle and bustle of daily life. This transition from corporate employee to lifestyle entrepreneur showcases the pursuit of personal well-being as a business model.

The American Dream Reimagined

The American Dream, historically characterized by the pursuit of prosperity and success through hard work in a land of opportunity, has evolved significantly over time. This transformation reflects changes in our society, economy, and individual aspirations. In recent years, entrepreneurship has emerged as a central element of the American Dream, symbolizing the quest for financial stability, personal fulfillment, independence, and the ability to impact the world.

Traditionally, the American Dream centered on the idea of upward mobility and success, often measured in terms of home ownership, stable employment, and a better standard of living than previous generations. With the shift in the economic landscape, traditional paths have become less certain, and the definition of success has broadened. Today, the American Dream has morphed into creating one's own path and living a life aligned with personal values and passions. Entrepreneurship stands ready to birth this modern interpretation of the American Dream by offering an avenue for individuals to achieve financial independence through creativity, innovation, and self-direction. It is a key component of the American Dream.

> **Today, the American Dream has morphed into creating one's own path and living a life aligned with personal values and passions.**

The rise of the digital age has made entrepreneurship more accessible, while a growing disillusionment with the corporate ladder makes it most appealing. The ability to start a business from anywhere with relatively low initial costs has democratized the process, positioning entrepreneurship as a viable and attractive option for achieving the American Dream and escaping the confines of traditional employment. Innovation, hard work, and the pursuit of happiness continue to be part of the pioneer spirit.

Business startups are often at the forefront of innovation. They fill niches that larger corporations may overlook. The unique insights and passions of entrepreneurs who are free to experiment and push boundaries in ways that larger entities cannot drive this innovation. This spirit of innovation not only contributes to the economy but also the social fabric, bringing new ideas and solutions to life.

Much like the early settlers of this country, the journey of building a business from the ground up rests in the arms of hard work. Business owners often wear multiple hats, managing everything from product development to marketing and sales. Hard work motivated by a commitment to a vision and the satisfaction of creating something meaningful built our country and still builds businesses today.

The pursuit of happiness is foundational to the American Dream. Adams and Jefferson knew it in the 1700s, and entrepreneurs recognize it today. Entrepreneurship provides a sense of purpose and fulfillment that goes beyond financial rewards. For many, the ability to make a living by doing what they love is the ultimate realization of the American Dream.

Entrepreneurship has become a cornerstone of personal and financial freedom. Business ownership embodies the bedrock of the American Dream, offering a deeply personal and universally inspiring path to success.

The Psychological and Emotional Journey

The journey into entrepreneurship is as much a psychological and emotional voyage as a professional one. Success in this realm demands more than just a viable business idea or a robust market strategy; it requires significant shifts in mindset coupled with the emotional resilience to navigate the rollercoaster of highs and lows that define the entrepreneurial experience. The transformation from working nine-to-five to being a business owner will require a heightened awareness of your emotional well-being.

Moving from the security of a regular paycheck requires embracing uncertainty as an opportunity for growth and innovation. Rather than keeping a fixed mindset, where challenges seem like insurmountable obstacles, entrepreneurs have to move to a growth mindset, where we see challenges as opportunities to learn and improve. Without this mental shift, the entrepreneurial journey can take a toll on your emotions.

Like pioneers of old, entrepreneurs cultivate the ability to bounce back. While this might seem tough at first, resilience can be built by facing challenges head-on and learning from experience. The entrepreneurial landscape is constantly evolving, with market trends, consumer preferences, and technology shifting rapidly. Success also requires an adaptable mindset, willingness to pivot strategies, embrace new ideas, and let go of approaches that no longer serve the business's objectives. This flexibility can be the difference between stagnation and growth.

One of the psychological and emotional hurdles entrepreneurs face is fear. Perhaps the most pervasive among new entrepreneurs is the fear of failure. This fear can be paralyzing, preventing individuals from taking necessary risks or even starting their venture. Entrepreneurs learn to accept failure as a part of the learning process and focus on the journey rather than solely on the outcome.

Stepping into the world of entrepreneurship also brings many challenges. Financial insecurity, overwhelm, burnout, and isolation top the list. The fear of failure feeds the uncertainty of the early stages of business. Planning, budgeting, and having a financial safety net can alleviate financial insecurity. Additionally, diversifying income streams and being proactive in financial management can help navigate periods of economic instability.

Successful entrepreneurs must develop time management strategies, learn to delegate tasks, and prioritize self-care to maintain their health and well-being. Self-care includes building a support network of fellow entrepreneurs, mentors, and advisors.

The mountains and valleys of entrepreneurship can take a toll. Fortunately, many strategies have been developed to help manage stress, maintain a positive outlook, and keep motivation high even in the face of adversity.

The psychological and emotional journey of entrepreneurship is fraught with challenges, but it is also ripe with opportunities for personal growth and achievement. By cultivating resilience, adaptability, and a willingness to take calculated risks, entrepreneurs can navigate the complexities of this path. Addressing fears and challenges with practical strategies and a supportive community can pave the way for a fulfilling and successful entrepreneurial journey, transforming obstacles into catalysts for growth and innovation.

Preparing for the Leap

Preparing for the leap into entrepreneurship involves careful planning, introspection, and strategic thinking. This preparation sets the foundation for a successful business venture and helps mitigate the risks associated with entrepreneurship. Entrepreneurship is not a one-size-fits-all solution.

Before diving into entrepreneurship, evaluate your motivations, strengths, weaknesses, and tolerance for risk. Understanding why you want to start a business and whether you possess the necessary attributes, such as resilience, adaptability, and determination, can help gauge your readiness for the entrepreneurial journey.

As you move into the realm of entrepreneurship, you'll also need to set clear, achievable goals to help you maintain focus and motivation, breaking down the overwhelming task of building a business into manageable steps. A comprehensive business plan can give you this roadmap, serve as a guide, and communicate your vision to potential partners or investors.

Your business plan should include an executive summary, company description, market analysis, organization and management structure, product or service line, marketing and sales strategies, funding requests (if applicable), financial projections, and an appendix with supporting documents.

This won't be the last time you consult your business plan. This living document will evolve as your business grows and market conditions change. Regularly revisiting and updating your plan will help you stay aligned with your goals and adapt to new challenges.

Entrepreneurs also need a continuous learning mindset. First, you'll want to identify your skills and those you need to develop. By prioritizing the need to gain knowledge and skills, you improve your business acumen, boost confidence, and reduce the fear of the unknown. Entrepreneurship often requires a jack-of-all-trades approach, especially in the early stages. However, recognizing areas where additional training or support is needed can prevent potential roadblocks.

Identify your skills and those you need to develop.

The preparation stage also means evaluating your financial status. You'll want to build a financial cushion before you leave your steady paycheck behind. Aim to save enough to cover personal living expenses for at least six to twelve months. This safety net allows for focus on the business without the immediate pressure of generating income.

During this stage, entrepreneurs begin developing a detailed budget and identifying sources for initial capital. You'll need to estimate the amount your business will require to get started, such as legal, accounting, licensing, inventory, equipment, and marketing. You might consider your personal savings, loans, or investors, and you'll need to understand the implications of each.

To address the psychological and emotional aspects of this transformation, it's vital to practice self-care. This includes recognizing that setbacks do not reflect personal failure but are just part of the entrepreneurial process. Practicing self-compassion can help maintain mental and emotional well-being through the ups and downs.

Preparing for the leap into entrepreneurship demands a holistic approach that encompasses personal and financial readiness, thorough market research, strategic choice of a business model, and the development of a detailed business plan. This preparation is not just about mitigating risks but also about positioning yourself and your business for success. By taking these steps, aspiring entrepreneurs can navigate the transition more smoothly, setting a strong foundation for the exciting journey ahead.

Key Takeaways

- **The American Dream has morphed into the Entrepreneurial Dream.** The allure of entrepreneurship represents a viable alternative to traditional employment and offers individuals the chance to break free from the constraints of a nine-to-five.

- **Transitioning from employee to entrepreneur requires preparation and offers many challenges and rewards.** You'll need a significant shift in mindset as well as resilience to make the transformation from paycheck to freedom. The leap will require financial planning, skills and knowledge, market research, and a supportive network.

- **Entrepreneurship requires deep commitment.** This is more than just starting a business; it's embarking on a journey of self-discovery, facing and overcoming challenges, and making an impact on your community. Candidates need a clear vision and a willingness to navigate the ups and downs of the entrepreneurial world.

- **Entrepreneurship presents the freedom to pursue passions.** Entrepreneurs have the flexibility to design their own lives and the potential for financial independence. This journey can become the pathway to personal development and ultimate fulfillment.

2

Finding Your Fit:
Selecting the Right Business

The journey to entrepreneurship starts with selecting a business that has the potential for success and aligns with your vision and goals. Identifying the ideal franchise or business opportunity requires a strategic approach, considering several factors that can influence your venture's immediate and long-term success.

Understand Yourself

Begin by conducting a thorough self-assessment to help you understand your values, strengths, weaknesses, passions, and aversions. This introspective analysis will help you narrow down potential businesses that align with your skills and interests, making your day-to-day operations more fulfilling and sustainable in the long run.

Start by listing your strengths. These could include specific skills like leadership, communication, and financial management or more general attributes such as resilience, creativity, or the ability to work under pressure. Recognizing your strengths can help you identify business opportunities that capitalize on what you do best. For instance, a business that requires team management and customer interaction may be ideal if you have strong leadership and communication skills.

Understanding the places that cause frustration can prevent future challenges in running your business.

Equally important is acknowledging your weaknesses. Be honest about areas you may need to develop or recruit support. Understanding the places that cause frustration can prevent future challenges in running your business. Identifying these areas early on allows you to seek business opportunities that require minimal involvement in your weaker areas or provide support systems that can help mitigate these weaknesses. For example, if financial management isn't your strong suit, looking for a franchise with a robust accounting and financial support system might be beneficial.

Next, make a list of things you are truly passionate about. A business that aligns with your interests will likely keep you motivated, especially when facing challenges. Reflect on activities you enjoy and how these could translate into business opportunities. Your passion can also be a strong selling point to customers. When you are passionate about your work, you're more likely to immerse yourself fully in the business, leading to greater creativity and innovation. This heightened engagement can translate into developing unique products or services, enhancing customer experience, and identifying new market opportunities. For example, a passion for healthy living might lead you to consider a health food franchise or a fitness center.

Just as critical as knowing your passions is understanding your aversions. Which aspects of business ownership do you dislike or struggle with? Steer clear of business models that heavily involve those elements. For instance, a bar or restaurant franchise might not be the best fit if you prefer not to deal with high customer turnover or late hours.

Lastly, you need to make sure your business choice aligns with your financial objectives. Consider the initial investment required, the potential return on investment, and the time frame for achieving profitability. Be realistic about your financial expectations and seek opportunities that offer the potential to meet or exceed these goals.

Fortunately, you can find many tools and resources for self-assessment online. Personality tests, career aptitude tests, and even professional assessments designed to identify entrepreneurial aptitudes can assist you as you understand your personal vision and values. Additionally, consider consulting with a career coach or mentor who can provide an objective view of your skills and interests. This outside perspective can be incredibly valuable.

After your initial self-assessment, take time for reflection. Research industries or business models that align with your identified strengths and passions. This phase can include attending industry seminars, networking with professionals in your areas of interest, and reading up on potential business opportunities.

Finally, list the attributes of your ideal business based on your strengths, weaknesses, passions, and aversions. Then you can use this list as a guide when evaluating potential business opportunities. Aligning your entrepreneurial venture with your self-assessment increases the likelihood of long-term fulfillment and success and sets the stage for a future that deeply resonates with who you are and what you aim to achieve.

Understand the Market

Many factors play into the success of a business, and these variables look different depending on your location, population, and culture of the area. When considering the best business for your personality as well as your community, consider the fact that some industries weather economic downturns better than others, making them more resilient and potentially safer investments. Healthcare, essential services, and digital products have historically shown resilience during economic fluctuations. Assessing an industry's performance during past economic cycles can provide insights into its stability and long-term viability. This analysis can help you choose a business more likely to sustain itself through varied economic conditions.

Additionally, look for industries showing signs of expansion. This could be through increased consumer demand, technological innovations, or new government policies supporting the industry. Expansion can indicate a healthy market with room for new entrants. For instance, the rise of digital commerce and telehealth services has seen significant growth, driven by technological advancements and changes in consumer preferences.

As you consider what kind of business you might like to build, assess how easily each business can adapt to changing market demands. Flexibility in your business model, product line, or service offerings can be a significant advantage in responding to future market trends and long-term success.

Is your business idea based on a fleeting trend, or does it fulfill a long-term need? Focusing on products or services with enduring demand can mitigate the risk of market shifts rendering your business obsolete.

Underserved markets represent opportunities to meet unfulfilled customer needs. Conducting surveys, focus groups, or analyzing search engine data can help identify areas where consumer demand is not adequately met by current offerings. Entering an underserved market can allow you to carve out a niche, thereby reducing competition and establishing your business as a go-to provider for that specific need. Plus, high-margin products or services can offer more flexibility and potential for profitability.

After you choose the area of business you'd like to pursue, you'll need to **Assessing the market demand for the products or services you intend to offer is crucial.** identify your target audience, understand their needs, and determine how your product or service meets those needs. Assessing the market demand for the products or services you intend to offer is crucial. A business that meets a persistent need or solves a common problem is more likely to succeed. Consider the current demand and potential future trends that could affect your business. This can include technological advancements, shifts in consumer behavior, regulatory changes, and socioeconomic factors. Identifying and understanding these trends can help you anticipate changes in demand and adapt your business model accordingly. Utilize industry reports, market analysis, and demographic data to inform your decision-making process. This research should inform your marketing strategies and product development.

You'll also need to analyze your competitors to understand their strengths and weaknesses, market position, and customer perceptions. Look at their sales volumes, customer reviews, and market share. A high level of competition might indicate strong demand, but this also requires you to make your offering stand out to capture market share. This information can also help you identify market gaps. Your competition can help you identify resilient and expanding sectors, as well as those underserved in your target market.

Identifying your audience, market trends, and areas with growth potential is just the beginning of your market research. As you grow, you'll want to keep abreast of emerging market trends. This involves monitoring industry news, reading reports from market research firms, and following thought leaders and influencers within specific sectors. Trends can indicate shifting consumer behaviors, technological advancements, or new regulatory environments that could open up opportunities or present challenges for businesses. For instance, the growing emphasis on sustainability and eco-friendly products has spurred growth in green technologies and organic food markets.

Comprehensive industry reports and market analysis are invaluable for understanding the competitive landscape, key players, market size, and growth forecasts. These reports can also provide insights into customer demographics, preferences, and behaviors. Resources like IBISWorld, Statista, and Euromonitor offer detailed reports on various industries and markets.

Demographic data will help you tailor your business to the specific needs of your target market. Look at your potential customers' age, income, education level, and lifestyle preferences. This information can guide you in choosing a business that aligns with their needs. Government agencies, market research firms, Google trends, social media analytics tools, and industry-specific databases can provide rich demographic insights.

Networking with professionals in your industry of interest can offer real-world insights that reports and data might not capture. Industry conferences, seminars, and online forums are excellent places to connect with seasoned entrepreneurs who can share their experiences, challenges, and advice on navigating the market. The research phase is a critical component of the business selection process, providing a foundation of knowledge to base your entrepreneurial decisions.

By thoroughly investigating market trends, industry resilience, expanding sectors, and underserved markets, you will equip yourself with the information needed to identify a business opportunity with strong growth potential. This informed approach will enable you to align your business venture with market realities, significantly increasing your chances of success in the competitive landscape of entrepreneurship.

Assessing market demand is a multi-faceted process that involves understanding current consumer needs, analyzing competitors, evaluating market size and growth, and anticipating future trends. By thoroughly researching and analyzing market demand, entrepreneurs can make informed decisions about the viability of their business ideas. This careful consideration ensures that the selected business meets a current market need and is positioned for adaptability and growth in the face of future market changes.

Understand the Financial Aspects

Potential business owners can be discouraged by the financial aspect of the entrepreneurial journey. These fears can often be alleviated by the costs compared to the possible income.

Start by identifying your financial goals.

- Are they more immediate?

- Do you need to generate a steady income within the first year, or are your financial needs more long-term?

- Do you have time to build a scalable business you will eventually sell or pass down? This distinction can influence the type of business you choose and your strategy for growth.

Begin by listing the comprehensive upfront costs involved in starting the business. For a franchise, this includes franchise fees, if applicable, equipment and inventory costs, initial marketing and branding expenses, and any required renovations or leasehold improvements.

Next, you'll compare these costs against your available capital to determine feasibility and explore various funding options, such as savings, loans, investors, or crowdfunding. Each option has considerations regarding repayment terms, interest rates, and equity sharing. Ensure the chosen funding method aligns with your long-term financial health and business ownership goals.

In addition to upfront costs, you'll need a projection of expenses to run your business. Consider both fixed costs, such as rent and salaries, as well as variable costs, such as the cost of goods sold and marketing expenses.

After you've made a realistic list of your projected expenses, develop a list of feasible revenue projections based on market research, competitor analysis, and pricing strategies. Factor in the time it typically takes for a business in your chosen industry to become profitable, considering any seasonal variations or market trends that may impact sales.

With your projected costs and revenue lists complete, you can calculate potential profit margins by subtracting expected expenses from revenue. This allows you to plan for effective cash flow management, especially in the early stages of the business. Maintaining a healthy cash flow is critical for covering operational expenses and sustaining the business until it becomes profitable. Plus, you can perform a break-even analysis to determine how long it will take for your business to cover its initial investment and start generating profit. This timeline should align with your financial planning and the level of financial risk you're prepared to take.

Your financial expectations must align with market realities. Research the average income for businesses in your chosen sector and region. Understand that achieving significant profitability may take time and requires patience and persistence. This means you'll also want to assess your risk tolerance to determine how much financial uncertainty you can comfortably manage. Starting a business involves inherent risks, and it's crucial to clearly understand your capacity to handle potential financial challenges.

Choose the Right Business for Your Lifestyle

Different business models affect lifestyles and have varied location needs. Some businesses require a physical storefront, while others operate remotely. From small offices to warehouses, as well as the population required to sustain your business choice, consider each aspect as you move from paycheck to freedom. And make sure your business choice complements your desired lifestyle and allows for a healthy work-life balance.

Brick-and-mortar establishments, like restaurants or retail stores, not only demand a physical presence, they also influence location based on market demographics and foot traffic, narrowing your housing choices. In contrast, online businesses offer flexibility in location, potentially allowing you to live anywhere with a reliable internet connection.

The accessibility of your target market will also influence your lifestyle and location. Businesses that rely on local clientele need a location with a high concentration of their target demographic. This consideration may require you to relocate or commute, impacting your lifestyle.

Additionally, local zoning laws and business regulations can significantly influence where you can operate your business. Compliance might limit your options and necessitate adjustments to your lifestyle or living arrangements.

It's vital that your self-assessment include what you want your work-life balance to look like immediately and within the next five to ten years. How much control do you want to have over your schedule? Some businesses demand more than the standard forty-hour workweek, especially during the startup phase. Consider whether you're willing to make personal sacrifices in the short term for long-term gains. Owning a business often offers autonomy; however, certain types of businesses require you to be present during specific hours or seasons. If flexibility is a priority, seek business models that allow you to set your own schedule.

High-pressure environments may affect your health and personal life.

You'll also need to consider the stress levels associated with different types of businesses and your tolerance for stress. High-pressure environments may affect your health and personal life. Choose a business that aligns with your stress management capabilities and contributes positively to your overall well-being.

Finally, list your personal values. Is environmental sustainability important to you? If so, you'll want to research business models with low environmental impact or contribute positively to environmental causes.

You'll also want to take into consideration your life phase and think about changes you foresee. Would you like to start a family or retire in the next five years? Your business choice should be flexible enough to accommodate these future lifestyle changes.

Finding the perfect business fit is not just about tapping into market potential; it's about creating a harmonious blend of personal fulfillment, financial success, and positive societal impact. By carefully navigating these considerations, entrepreneurs can embark on a journey that is not only financially rewarding but also deeply satisfying and aligned with their broader life aspirations.

Understand How Business Startups Influence the Economy

New businesses play a pivotal role in the economy, serving as the backbone of local and national markets worldwide. For instance, business startups are significant job creators, often cited as the primary source of new jobs in many economies. These businesses help reduce unemployment rates and provide livelihoods for local residents. More than just numbers on a chart, these businesses represent opportunities for individuals to build careers, support families, and achieve personal goals. Business startups frequently offer more personalized, flexible work environments, which can be more appealing to a diverse workforce and can contribute to higher levels of job satisfaction.

Innovation is the lifeblood of economic growth, and new businesses are at the forefront of innovative practices. Their size allows them to be nimble, allowing them to adapt quickly to market changes and customer needs. Startups often push the boundaries of their industries, introducing new products, services, and technologies. This innovation drives competition, compelling larger businesses to innovate as well, and contributes to the overall dynamism of the economy.

Innovation is the lifeblood of economic growth.

Business startups contribute significantly to the identity and development of their communities. Their unique products and services reflect the character and needs of the community, enhancing its appeal and vitality. They often help preserve local traditions and cultures while also fostering a sense of community pride and belonging. These business owners often spearhead local initiatives, supporting schools, charities, and community events, which enriches the social fabric of the area.

By diversifying the economic base, local businesses contribute to the stability and growth of their immediate and national economies. They buffer against economic downturns because they are less likely to enact large-scale layoffs than larger corporations. Additionally, these businesses stimulate economic growth by generating revenue that circulates within their community, supporting other businesses and services, and amplifying the impact of every dollar. This multiplier effect leads to greater overall economic health and resilience.

Entrepreneurial businesses also contribute to the diversification of the marketplace by catering to a wide array of cultural, demographic, and personal preferences. This inclusivity not only enriches the market but also ensures that more communities and consumer needs are represented and met. Entrepreneurs from varied backgrounds bring different perspectives and solutions to the table, fostering innovation and resilience in the economy.

The role of business startups in the economy cannot be overstated. They are crucial for job creation, innovation, community development, economic stability, and growth. Local business ownership offers a way for individuals to contribute positively to their communities and the broader economy while achieving personal and financial freedom. By understanding the significance of businesses, policymakers, consumers, and budding entrepreneurs can better support these vital entities, ensuring a robust, dynamic, and inclusive economy.

Understand the Legal and Regulatory Environment

As you choose your business type and model, it's vital to be aware of the legal and regulatory implications of your chosen business. Some industries may be heavily regulated, requiring additional investments in compliance and legal support. Understanding these requirements upfront can prevent costly surprises down the road.

Navigating the legal and regulatory environment is a crucial step in selecting the right business. Compliance with laws and regulations not only ensures your business operates within legal boundaries but also protects it from potential fines, legal disputes, and reputational damage. Here's a deeper look into understanding and managing your business venture's legal and regulatory aspects.

You'll want to consider industry-specific regulations. Healthcare, food service, and financial entities face stringent regulatory scrutiny compared to other sectors. Regardless of your business choice, look at licensing requirements, safety standards, and consumer protection laws.

And though we highly recommend networking and learning from others in your industry, remember that legal requirements can vary significantly from jurisdiction to jurisdiction. Both national and local regulations can affect your business. This includes zoning laws, business licensing, and employment laws.

If your business involves manufacturing, waste disposal, or the use of hazardous materials, you'll need to be aware of environmental regulations. Compliance in this area prevents legal issues and demonstrates your commitment to sustainability, an increasingly important factor for consumers.

Compliance with these laws can entail significant costs, including the price of hiring legal counsel or compliance specialists. With the complexity of legal and regulatory environments, consulting with legal professionals specializing in your industry can be invaluable. They can provide tailored advice, assist with license applications, and help navigate any legal challenges. Factor these costs into your business plan to ensure you have the financial resources to meet all legal obligations. Many government agencies and industry associations also offer compliance resources and guidance for businesses. These can be excellent starting points for understanding your legal obligations and finding reputable legal advisors.

These legal advisors can also help with business agreements and contracts, including those with customers, suppliers, and employees. Well-drafted contracts can protect your business interests and clarify the rights and responsibilities of all parties involved.

Appropriate insurance coverage can also help mitigate risks associated with liabilities. This can include general liability insurance, professional liability insurance, product liability insurance, and industry-specific insurance, depending on your business type.

Legal and regulatory landscapes are not static; they evolve in response to technological advances, societal changes, and policy shifts. Implement a system that will keep you updated on relevant laws and regulations to ensure ongoing compliance. Understanding and managing the legal and regulatory environment is essential for any business venture. Early identification of applicable laws and regulations, careful planning for compliance, and seeking expert advice can prevent legal issues and ensure your business operates smoothly. This proactive approach protects your business and builds trust with customers, employees, and partners by demonstrating your commitment to legal and ethical standards. Integrating legal compliance into your business planning and operations sets a solid foundation for long-term success and credibility in your chosen industry.

Key Takeaways

- **Do a thorough self-assessment.** This introspective process is crucial for narrowing down the types of businesses that align with personal skills and interests and promise greater job satisfaction and resilience in the face of entrepreneurial challenges.

- **Research various business types and models.** Identify industries with growth potential and understand the dynamics of market demand. Then, select a business that meets a persistent need or addresses a common problem.

- **Develop a plan to stay on top of the legal and regulatory environment.** It's imperative to comply with industry-specific regulations and local and national laws.

3

Don't Recreate the Wheel

Your Best Bet Is Owning a Franchise

The journey from employment to entrepreneurship offers numerous opportunities, each offering its own set of challenges and rewards. Franchising stands out as a distinctive bridge combining the structure of traditional employment with the independence of business ownership. It also presents a compelling option for aspiring entrepreneurs seeking a balanced approach to starting a business venture.

Franchising allows individuals to operate their businesses while leveraging the support and proven systems of an established brand. This unique model provides a blend of autonomy and guidance, making it an attractive option for those transitioning from a W2 employment mindset to the entrepreneurial world. Unlike starting a business from scratch and navigating the uncertain waters of market validation and brand building, franchising lets entrepreneurs hit the ground running.

Is Franchising for You?

Before embarking on this journey, evaluate whether franchising aligns with your entrepreneurial vision and goals. Franchising offers a unique blend of entrepreneurship and partnership, so it is essential to assess how well this model fits with your aspirations, lifestyle, and business approach.

The first step is to discover what business type fits your personality and vision. New business owners must consider personal goals and other factors when deciding which path to take. Entrepreneurial aspirations vary widely—some may seek the creative freedom of starting a new business, while others may prefer the structured support of a franchise. If you thrive on creating everything from scratch, you might prefer the autonomy of traditional entrepreneurship.

On the other hand, if you enjoy a proven framework, you should opt for structure, and a franchise might be the answer. The innovative personality likes to disrupt markets, while the optimizer excels in executing within an established model like a franchise.

Autonomy vs. Structure: Do you thrive on creating everything from scratch or prefer operating within a proven framework?

Innovation vs. Optimization: Is your focus on innovating and disrupting markets, or do you excel in optimizing and executing within an established model?

Your financial, lifestyle, and legacy goals can help determine whether a franchise better fits your business model than more traditional entrepreneurship. Matching your goals with the realities of franchising can highlight whether this path can fulfill your aspirations.

Financial Objectives: What are your income expectations, and how does franchising fit your financial planning?

Lifestyle Goals: How does owning a business fit with your desired lifestyle, work-life balance, and personal commitments?

Impact and Legacy: Do you want to make a specific impact in your community or industry? Does a particular franchise align with these values?

If you've decided to own a franchise rather than start a traditional business, you need to decide which opportunity you want to take advantage of. Before you choose a franchise, you must do your due diligence. It takes research to determine which franchise best fits your vision, values, and personality. This research phase is critical to understanding what to expect and whether a particular franchise offers the right fit for your vision.

Questions to Consider When Choosing a Franchise

- **Brand Alignment:** Does the franchise's brand values, market position, and customer base align with your vision?

- **Financial Performance:** Review the Franchise Disclosure Document (FDD) for earnings claims, financial health, and startup costs. Does the financial model meet your expectations and investment capacity?

- **Support Structure:** Evaluate the franchisor's training, support, and resources. Are they sufficient to meet your needs and help you overcome potential challenges?

Regardless of what kind of business you decide to start, you'll need to analyze the market. A thorough market analysis can reveal whether the business or franchise opportunity you choose is viable and if it aligns with your vision for growth and success. Industry trends can also influence your decision; certain sectors may lend themselves better to franchising and others to fresh, innovative startups.

Market Demand: Is there a sustained demand for the products or services? How does the franchise perform in various economic conditions?

Competition: Does the franchise's offering stand out in the local competitive landscape?

Trends and Growth: Could emerging trends impact the franchise positively or negatively? Is the industry growing?

Finally, your research should provide enough information to assess your compatibility with and readiness to commit to a franchise.

Operational Compatibility: Are you comfortable with the day-to-day operations and customer interactions typical for the franchise?

Commitment Level: Franchising is a long-term commitment. Are you ready to invest the necessary time, energy, and resources to build a successful franchise?

Adaptability: Are you prepared to adapt to the franchisor's system and business model or market changes?

The Pros and Cons of Different Business Types

Choosing franchising—or any form of business ownership—should be informed and strategic. Franchising is not a one-size-fits-all solution, but it can serve as an ideal stepping stone for many. The first step is to decide if a franchise is right for you. Each path offers unique advantages and challenges.

	Pros	Cons
Starting a New Business	Freedom Limitless Potential Cost Flexibility	High Risk Resource Intensity Operational Challenges
Acquire an Existing Business	Immediate Operation Established Market Presence Proven Business Model	Substantial Investment Inherited Problems Lack of Flexibility
Buy Into a Franchise	Brand Recognition Proven Business Model Support and Training Easier Financing	Franchise Fees & Royalties Operational Restrictions Brand Dependency

Many people first consider starting a new business when they dream of becoming entrepreneurs. They like the idea of complete control and the freedom to build their vision without restraints. These entrepreneurs have no cap on the potential for growth and expansion, offering exciting possibilities for innovation. The initial costs for a business startup can vary depending on the business model and how much you plan to scale at launch. You can prepare for a lean start to keep costs down.

Building systems and processes from the ground up requires substantial effort and expertise.

Unfortunately, new businesses face high uncertainty with no established customer base or market presence and have a high level of resource intensity. Entrepreneurs must invest significant time and resources into market research, brand development, and customer acquisition. Building systems and processes from the ground up requires substantial effort and expertise.

If you choose to acquire an existing business, you can begin operations immediately. Assuming you purchased a business with a good reputation, you won't have to build a customer base because you'll have one built in. You will also inherit a proven business model that can provide insights into the viability and future performance. The downside to acquiring an established business is the significant upfront cost, potential inherited problems such as debts or poor employee morale, and the lack of flexibility in changing the existing business model or brand perception.

Franchising has its own set of pros and cons. Franchisees list fees and royalties as one of the top cons because these funds can impact profit margins. Franchise agreements also include operational restrictions that may limit the entrepreneur's ability to make certain business decisions, affecting creativity and independence. Finally, your success as a franchisee depends on the franchisor's brand. Negative publicity for the chain can affect the franchisee's business.

The Front Door Advantages of Franchising

On the other hand, franchising offers unique advantages, making it an attractive option for aspiring entrepreneurs navigating the complexities of starting a business. One of the most significant benefits of franchising is the instant access to built-in brand recognition. Established franchises come with a loyal customer base, reducing the time and effort needed to build trust and attract business. This recognition can lead to quicker sales and profitability compared to starting a brand from scratch. When consumers face the choice of patronizing a well-known franchise or an unknown new business, they more often opt for the familiar. This inherent trust is a product of the franchise's history, its consistency in product or service quality, and its established presence in the market. For a new franchisee, this means that the battle for credibility, often the steepest hill for new businesses, has already been won. The brand's reputation precedes itself, allowing franchisees to focus on maintaining and enhancing customer experience rather than starting from the ground up.

> And profitability compared to starting a brand from scratch. When consumers face the choice of patronizing a well-known franchise or an unknown new business, they more often opt for the familiar.

Built-in brand recognition also reduces the need for extensive marketing efforts. While localized marketing is still important, franchisees benefit from national advertising campaigns and brand-wide promotions that individual business owners would find prohibitively expensive. This collective marketing effort not only supports the individual franchisee but also strengthens the brand as a whole, creating a positive feedback loop of brand reinforcement and customer loyalty.

Having an initial customer base can also accelerate the path to profitability. New businesses often face a slow start as they work to attract customers and build their market presence. In contrast, consumers' pre-existing familiarity and trust in the brand can create a quicker start, allowing franchisees to recoup their initial investment faster and potentially reinvest in growth opportunities sooner than they might have been able to otherwise.

Brand equity, or the value derived from consumer perception of the brand, is a second powerful asset that franchisees inherit. This includes the tangible aspects of the product or service and the emotional connections and loyalty customers feel towards the brand. Franchisees can leverage this equity to introduce new products or services more effectively, participate in brand-wide loyalty programs, and benefit from the overall positive sentiment towards the brand. This equity, built up over the years by the franchisor and other franchisees, provides a competitive edge that is difficult for new businesses to replicate.

The Back Door Advantages of Franchising

Franchising provides access to a tested and refined business model. If you choose to own a franchise, you'll get proven operational practices that have been optimized for efficiency, cost-effectiveness, and customer satisfaction. Franchisees avoid common pitfalls because the operational roadmap shortens the learning curve.

Marketing is critical to the success of any business, but it can be one of the most challenging areas for new entrepreneurs. Franchisors have developed proven marketing strategies that have been tested and refined across different demographics and regions. These strategies include national advertising campaigns, local marketing initiatives, online presence, and social media engagement. By leveraging the brand's marketing resources and expertise, franchisees can effectively reach their target audience, promote their offerings, and drive customer engagement without the trial and error that standalone businesses often face.

In addition to the marketing strategies franchisors provide, franchisees can take advantage of national advertising efforts, seasonal promotions, and local marketing templates and guidelines. By pooling resources, franchisees benefit from high-impact marketing campaigns that extend beyond the reach of individual business owners, increasing visibility and attracting customers.

Franchises also benefit from a continuous product development and innovation pipeline, ensuring the business stays relevant and competitive. Franchisors invest significant resources in researching and developing new products or services, testing them in various markets, and rolling them out across the franchise network. This access to a stream of new offerings allows franchisees to refresh their inventory or service portfolio, meet evolving customer needs, and generate additional revenue streams without bearing the full cost and risk of development themselves.

These products and services also often include proprietary software and systems that streamline operations, from sales and customer relationship management (CRM) to inventory and employee scheduling. The result of significant research and **Customer satisfaction is at the heart of any successful business.** development investments by the franchisor, this technology provides a competitive edge by optimizing efficiency and productivity, freeing up time to focus on growth and customer service.

Customer satisfaction is at the heart of any successful business, and franchisors understand this deeply. They provide franchisees with detailed customer service protocols designed to deliver a consistent, high-quality experience across all locations. These protocols cover everything from handling inquiries and managing complaints to loyalty programs and customer feedback mechanisms. Implementing these proven customer service practices helps franchisees build strong relationships with their customers, fostering loyalty and repeat business.

The most significant advantage of the franchising model is the reduction of uncertainty. Franchisees bypass the ambiguity and risk associated with starting a new business from scratch. Instead of experimenting to find a viable approach, the business owner can focus on executing a tested and effective strategy, optimizing their operations, and scaling their business. Plus, banks like the idea of reduced uncertainty.

Banks and financial institutions value the predictability and reliability of a well-established franchise brand. Because this track record reduces the perceived risk, lenders are more inclined to finance this type of business.

While support and training can be difficult for new business owners to develop, franchisors offer comprehensive support and training programs to ensure their franchisees are well-equipped to run their businesses. This can include initial training that will immerse the franchisee in the brand, as well as ongoing education on new products or services. Franchisees also have access to proprietary software or systems. This level of support can be invaluable for entrepreneurs new to the industry or business ownership, providing a safety net as they learn the ropes.

The learning doesn't stop after the doors open. Franchisors provide ongoing education to keep franchisees updated on new products, services, technologies, and market trends. This can include webinars, workshops, and regional meetings, offering opportunities for franchisees to continue their education and stay ahead in a competitive market.

Beyond training, franchisors provide ongoing operational support through field consultants or support staff. These professionals offer guidance on best practices, help troubleshoot issues, and advise on growth strategies. This hands-on support can be particularly beneficial for franchisees facing challenges or looking to expand their business.

It's a testament to the franchisor's commitment to each franchisee's success, ensuring they have direct access to expert advice and support when needed.

Finally, the franchise model fosters a unique network of peers—fellow franchisees who share the same goals and challenges. Veteran franchisees can offer insights and advice to newer members of the network, drawing on their own experiences with the brand, the market, and even specific operational challenges.

Franchisors often facilitate the network by providing online platforms where franchisees can exchange ideas, share best practices, and offer mutual support. This community aspect can be incredibly valuable, providing a rich tapestry of resources, camaraderie, and a pool of collective knowledge that franchisees can draw upon.

Regional meetings and national conferences also allow franchisees to connect with their peers. Franchisors use these venues to provide educational opportunities through workshops and seminars, create small group forums, and celebrate achievements within the system. This peer-to-peer support mechanism can give attendees a tangible sense of being part of a larger endeavor and allow them to learn from the successes and challenges of others.

Regional meetings and national conferences also allow franchisees to connect with their peers.

Franchises offer a structured path to business ownership that is supported at every step. This framework not only reduces the risks associated with starting a new business but also accelerates the learning curve. For many, this level of support is a deciding factor in choosing franchising as the route to entrepreneurship, providing the safety net and resources necessary to succeed in the competitive world of business.

The Financial Advantage to Franchises

We've already mentioned that banks like franchises because they are predictable. This type of business investment brings other financial benefits to the table. First, the perceived lower risk of the franchise means banks often give lower interest rates to franchise owners than traditional business startups. Because these rates directly affect the total cost of borrowing, this can create significant savings and allow for more manageable loan repayments.

Additionally, lenders typically extend higher loan amounts to franchisees for the same reasons they offer lower interest rates. A higher loan amount can be a game-changer for a franchisee, providing the funds to cover the initial franchise fee, startup costs, and working capital needed until the business becomes profitable. This financial flexibility enables franchisees to launch their businesses under optimal conditions, ensuring they have the resources necessary to succeed from the outset.

Longer repayment periods accompany lower interest rates and higher loan amounts. The lower monthly payments this affords are especially beneficial during the early stages of the business when cash flow might be tighter. Extending the loan's term reduces the immediate financial pressure, allowing the franchisee to focus on growing the business rather than just keeping up with loan repayments. This leads to a healthier financial situation, providing the breathing room needed to make strategic decisions that benefit the franchise's long-term success.

Some banks and financial institutions offer specialized financing programs tailored to prospective franchisees. These programs recognize the unique aspects of franchising and are designed to meet the specific needs of franchise business owners. Banks and financial institutions offering these programs often deeply understand the franchising model, including its operational, financial, and market dynamics. This expertise allows them to design customized loan products, such as lines of credit and deferred payment plans. Competitive terms and streamlined application processes are just a couple of ways banks align with the cash flow patterns and growth trajectories of franchised businesses.

Some franchisors partner with lenders to facilitate financing for their franchisees, further easing the process of securing necessary funds. These partnerships give franchisees access to financing options that are pre-approved or endorsed by the franchisor and allow the franchisor to attract more candidates to their franchise system. Lenders benefit because they can tap into a market of motivated and supported business owners, reducing their lending risk and capitalizing on the growth potential within the franchising sector.

Some franchisors partner with lenders to facilitate financing for their franchisees.

The combination of lower interest rates, higher loan amounts, and longer repayment periods creates an environment conducive to growth and development. With more favorable financing terms, franchisees can invest in marketing, staff training, and inventory. It also allows them to forecast their financial future more confidently, prepare more accurate budgets, and focus on other key areas that drive faster expansion, whether by opening additional locations, enhancing the customer experience, or adopting new technologies to improve efficiency.

The Collective Benefits

A cohesive network of franchisees can wield significant collective bargaining power when negotiating with suppliers and vendors. By pooling their needs, franchisees can secure more favorable terms, discounts, and exclusive deals that benefit their businesses. This collective approach to vendor relationships can lead to cost savings and improved product or service quality, enhancing the competitiveness and profitability of individual franchise locations.

The network of franchisees is a dynamic ecosystem providing more than support, education, collaboration, and a sense of belonging. The blend of tangible and intangible benefits and opportunities for collaboration enriches the franchising experience. By leveraging the full potential of this network, franchisees can propel their businesses to new heights.

The franchising model's potential for scale and growth is a significant draw for entrepreneurs. Their operational systems and processes are often designed for scalability and include specialized training. Some franchise owners open additional locations, while others use the advantages to scale operations within a single unit. Most franchisors typically have well-defined strategies for expansion, honed through the experience of growing their brand across various markets. They also offer training programs focused on multi-unit management and financial planning for expansion. Generally, franchise owners receive preferential terms for setting up more locations.

> The franchising model's potential for scale and growth is a significant draw for entrepreneurs.

This structured approach reduces the risk associated with scaling up, offering a clearer path to growth and making it easier for entrepreneurs to grow their businesses effectively and efficiently.

Success Stories

Many franchise owners begin their careers as employees within a fast-food franchise. Recognizing the potential for growth and driven by an entrepreneurial spirit, they decide to invest in their own franchise unit. Through dedication to customer service, operational efficiency, and a keen eye for market opportunities, they are able to expand their initial investment into ownership of multiple units within the same brand. These franchisees' success underscores the importance of understanding the operational side of the business and leveraging corporate support for expansion.

One inspiring case involves a franchisee who faced significant challenges in their initial foray into franchising, including market downturns and operational hurdles. By utilizing the franchisor's resources, adapting their business model to changing market conditions, and maintaining a focus on community engagement, they turned their struggling franchise into one of the top-performing units in the network. Their journey is a testament to the resilience required in franchising and the potential for turnaround with the right strategies and support.

Another particularly innovative franchisee took a unique approach to expanding their service-based franchise. They incorporated technology to enhance customer experience and streamline operations. Working closely with the franchisor to implement these changes significantly increased efficiency and customer satisfaction, leading to rapid growth and recognition within the franchise community. This story highlights the potential for franchisees to contribute to the evolution of the franchise system and achieve success through innovation.

A former corporate executive leveraged their experience in management and operations to transition into franchise ownership. Choosing a franchise aligned with their passion and skill set, they applied their corporate knowledge to optimize their operations and marketing strategies. Their professional background provided a solid foundation for understanding the complexities of business ownership, allowing them to scale quickly and become a leader within the franchise network.

Lastly, one franchisee started with a single unit and grew to own several, eventually taking on a mentorship role within the franchise network. Their ability to identify key growth opportunities, coupled with a commitment to mentoring new franchisees, has not only contributed to their personal success but has also strengthened the overall franchise system. This narrative emphasizes the value of community and support in the franchising model, illustrating how success can be both individual and collective and showcasing the full circle of franchising success.

These success stories illustrate the diverse paths to success in franchising, highlighting key themes such as resilience, innovation, effective use of support and resources, and the importance of community within the franchise network. Each story offers unique insights and lessons, providing inspiration and guidance for current and aspiring franchisees. The journeys of these successful franchise owners underscore the potential of franchising as a pathway to business ownership, growth, and personal fulfillment.

Key Takeaways

- **It's vital to understand your personality before choosing the business model you prefer.** Review the traits that fit a franchise owner best and the pros and cons of the different models.

- **Franchising offers many advantages,** such as built-in brand recognition, a customer base, networking, financial advantages, marketing, a proven business model, and more.

4

The Role of a Franchise Broker

Choosing the right franchise can be overwhelming. It's more than simply choosing a brand that seems appealing. Navigating this world requires a deep dive into the operational, financial, and strategic aspects of potential franchises to ensure alignment with the entrepreneur's goals and expectations. This is where the expertise of a franchise broker becomes invaluable.

Franchise brokers scrutinize the franchisor's support systems, including initial training programs, ongoing education, marketing support, and operational assistance. They evaluate whether these systems are robust enough to equip franchisees with the necessary tools and knowledge to succeed in their markets.

Because these professionals have a deep understanding of the franchising industry, including the various business models, opportunities available, and the intricacies of the franchise selection process, franchise brokers can help narrow the choices by using their expertise to evaluate the viability and potential of different franchises.

How a Franchise Broker Facilitates the Process of Business Ownership

The franchise broker's role is multifaceted and often begins with educating prospective franchisees regarding the benefits and risks as well as what to expect throughout the process. The broker walks them through the fundamentals of franchise structure, financial commitments, and legal considerations. This specialized knowledge provides a solid foundation for making informed decisions and sets realistic expectations. A significant part of their responsibility involves helping clients understand the intricacies of franchising. This education is pivotal, as it demystifies the process and empowers prospective entrepreneurs with the knowledge needed to navigate the franchising world confidently and make decisions that best align with their goals and capabilities.

A significant part of a franchise broker's responsibility involves helping clients under the intricacies of franchising.

Franchise brokers also provide tailored guidance based on the unique needs, interests, and financial capabilities of their clients. They help prospective franchisees find opportunities that fit their budget and align with their personal and professional goals, whether operating a hands-on, owner-operator business or a larger, management-oriented investment.

Understanding the risks involved in any business venture is crucial, and franchising is no exception. Franchise brokers play a crucial role in outlining the potential risks associated with franchising, including market saturation, the financial health of the franchisor, and the implications of the franchise agreement. They know the track record, satisfaction ratings, and availability of training and support of various franchises and can advise based on past performance. By providing a realistic assessment, brokers can help their clients take proactive steps to mitigate them, such as conducting thorough market research or seeking legal advice before signing a franchise agreement.

One of the most valuable aspects of enlisting the help of a franchise broker is the ability to set realistic expectations as far as the time and effort required to get a franchise off the ground, the typical timeframe for becoming profitable, and the ongoing responsibilities of a franchisee. This clarity helps prospective franchisees gauge their readiness and commitment to the franchising journey.

This foundation of understanding sets the stage for a more successful and fulfilling franchising experience, highlighting the significant value that professional guidance brings to business ownership.

Franchise Matchmakers

Personalized matchmaking is a cornerstone of the services offered by franchise brokers, distinguishing them as not just advisors but as pivotal partners in the journey toward entrepreneurship. By tailoring their recommendations, franchise brokers can significantly increase the likelihood of a successful and satisfying franchise partnership.

Franchise brokers begin the matchmaking process by developing a comprehensive profile of their clients. This profile includes not just financial information, such as investment budget and resources, but also personal preferences, lifestyle aspirations, professional background, and long-term goals. They also develop a snapshot of the client's risk tolerance. Understanding the client's complete picture helps brokers identify franchise opportunities that align with both the client's financial capacity and their vision for business ownership, ensuring a harmonious balance between work and life.

Understanding a client's business interests and goals is pivotal in the matchmaking process. Whether a client seeks a franchise that allows for passive ownership, wants to be directly involved in day-to-day operations, or aims to make a positive impact in their community, franchise brokers tailor their recommendations to meet these specific objectives. This goal-oriented approach ensures that clients are matched with franchises that not only meet their financial investment criteria but also fulfill their personal aspirations and professional ambitions.

Understanding a client's business interests and goals is pivotal in the matchmaking process.

Coupled with the broker's deep understanding of the franchising industry, including trends, growth sectors, and emerging opportunities, this dive into the client's needs allows the broker to provide informed recommendations that clients might not discover on their own. Their insight into the industry lets them assess the stability, growth potential, and support structure of various franchisors, ensuring that they match clients with franchises that have a solid foundation for success.

Personalized matchmaking is not a one-time event but an ongoing process that may involve reevaluating opportunities as the client's situation and the market evolve. Franchise brokers maintain an open line of communication, offering continued support and guidance as clients progress through the decision-making process, ensuring that the final choice remains the best fit over time.

Because they understand the obligations of both parties, franchise brokers play a part in conducting thorough due diligence, one of the most critical steps in choosing a franchise. These guides guide their clients through the review of Franchise Disclosure Documents (FDDs). The FDD contains essential information about the franchisor, including financial statements, litigation history, franchisee obligations, and the franchisor's obligations. A franchise broker helps prospective franchisees understand the implications of the FDD's disclosures, pointing out red flags or areas that require clarification.

The personalized matchmaking process employed by franchise brokers is instrumental in bridging the gap between prospective franchisees and their ideal business opportunities. By considering a holistic view of the client's financial capabilities, lifestyle preferences, business interests, and long-term goals, franchise brokers can significantly enhance the likelihood of a successful franchise partnership.

The Benefits of Professional Guidance in Finding a Franchise Fit

Choosing a franchise is a two-way commitment; it involves understanding what is expected from both the franchisee and the franchisor. Franchise brokers assist clients in comprehending the obligations outlined in the franchise agreement, such as initial and ongoing fees, marketing contributions, and operational standards. They help clients assess whether these obligations are reasonable and in line with industry norms, ensuring that prospective franchisees have a clear understanding of their commitments before signing any agreements.

With their industry knowledge, franchise brokers can significantly expedite the search process, saving prospective franchisees time and resources. They can filter through hundreds of opportunities to find those that meet specific criteria, streamlining the selection process.

The decision to pursue franchise ownership marks a pivotal moment in an entrepreneur's career, presenting immense opportunities and significant challenges. In this complex journey, the value of professional guidance cannot be overstated. A franchise broker serves as a guide and a strategic advisor.

A franchise broker has already addressed many of the foundational elements in selecting a business type we mentioned earlier. They can offer in-depth insight into market trends and industry dynamics and possess a broad understanding of various sectors, enabling them to identify industries with growth potential that match an entrepreneur's interests and investment capabilities.

Their research has given brokers detailed information on franchisors we recommend, including their market reputation, financial stability, and franchisee satisfaction levels. With a broker's help, you can easily shortlist franchises that fit your passions and purpose. They also

Brokers provide invaluable support during the negotiation process.

compare the compatibility of the franchise's culture and values with your own. This alignment is critical for long-term satisfaction and success in the franchise partnership.

Brokers also provide invaluable support during the negotiation process, ensuring clients secure the best possible terms for their franchise agreements. Franchise brokers draw on their extensive experience in the franchising industry to guide negotiations. They understand the norms and standards within the industry, including what terms can be negotiated and what concessions franchisors are likely to make. This knowledge enables them to advise clients on which terms are worth negotiating and how to present these requests effectively.

Effective communication is essential during franchise negotiations, so franchise brokers serve as intermediaries. They help articulate the franchisee's requests and concerns in a constructive and conducive manner to reach an agreement. This mediation can help maintain a positive relationship between the parties, laying the groundwork for a successful partnership. The broker's experience can lead to favorable outcomes that might be difficult to achieve independently.

Navigating Complex Agreements

Franchise agreements are often complex documents containing legal terminology and clauses that can be difficult for laypersons to understand. Franchise brokers help demystify these documents, explain the implications of various clauses, and identify any areas of concern. Their expertise can be invaluable in ensuring that franchisees fully understand the agreement they are entering into.

Ensuring a Smooth Closing Process

Once negotiations are successfully concluded, franchise brokers play a key role in facilitating the closing process. They ensure that all necessary documentation is in order, that agreed-upon terms are accurately reflected in the final franchise agreement, and that any remaining administrative hurdles are navigated smoothly. Their oversight during this phase helps ensure the transition into franchise ownership is seamless, allowing the new franchisee to focus on launching and growing their business.

As mentioned earlier, franchise brokers often have extensive networks within the franchising community, including connections to franchisors, existing franchisees, and financing sources. Access to this network can open doors to insights, testimonials, and funding opportunities that may not be readily available through independent research.

This broad industry coverage ensures prospective franchisees can explore ventures in areas they are passionate about or in markets they believe hold significant potential. Whether clients are interested in a niche market or a widely recognized brand, brokers can provide options that span the full spectrum of possibilities.

Various factors nuance the journey to finding the perfect franchise fit. Professional guidance offers manifold benefits in this process, including a shortcut through the maze of available options and a strategic partnership that enhances the likelihood of success. A franchise broker quickly becomes an indispensable asset in the quest for the right franchise opportunity.

One key benefit of working with a franchise broker is their ability to objectively assess franchisor track records. Unlike individual research, which may be influenced by marketing materials or personal biases, brokers offer an unbiased view based on factual data and industry standards. They can compare various franchisors within the same industry, pointing out differences in support, training, and financial performance. This objectivity helps prospective franchisees make informed decisions based on a balanced evaluation of potential risks and rewards.

Franchise brokers are also adept at identifying red flags that may not be apparent to individuals new to franchising. These red flags could include inconsistencies in financial statements, undisclosed legal disputes, or unrealistic earnings claims. By spotting these warning signs early in the selection process, brokers can steer clients away from potentially problematic franchises and towards opportunities with a more reliable and transparent operational history.

One of the most exciting aspects of working with a franchise broker is the potential to discover new or emerging franchises. These opportunities often offer lower initial investment costs, untapped market potential, and the chance to grow alongside a developing brand. Brokers are typically at the forefront of industry trends and can identify up-and-coming franchisors before they become widely known, giving their clients early access to lucrative opportunities.

Franchise brokers often know exclusive deals or terms unavailable to the general public. Through their industry relationships, they may be able to negotiate special arrangements, such as reduced franchise fees or more favorable terms for their clients. This inside access can make franchising more accessible for new entrepreneurs and increase the financial attractiveness of certain opportunities.

Franchise brokers often know exclusive deals or terms unavailable to the general public.

The sheer number of available options can be overwhelming for individuals new to franchising. A franchise broker's network acts as a curated collection of opportunities, streamlining the exploration process and making it more manageable. By leveraging the broker's network and knowledge, prospective franchisees can efficiently navigate the vast franchising landscape, focusing their energy on evaluating opportunities that truly align with their criteria.

Key Takeaways

- **Franchise brokers have an inside scoop on potential franchise opportunities.** It's impossible for the average entrepreneur to know about every available franchise opportunity. Franchise brokers specialize in keeping up-to-date with this information.

- **Franchise brokers specialize in getting to know you and your business goals.** These men and women know what questions to ask to help you complete the self-assessment we discussed previously. Understanding your passions, purpose, and pursuits proves invaluable when the broker begins matchmaking.

5

Tax Advantages of Business Ownership

Entrepreneurship inherently carries risks but offers unique financial rewards, including tax benefits not accessible to employees. These benefits are built into the tax code to encourage business investment, innovation, and growth. From deductions and credits for business expenses to specialized tax treatments for certain types of business income, the range of tax advantages available can significantly reduce an entrepreneur's taxable income and, by extension, their tax liability.

Owning a business brings more tax advantages than any other kind of investment. As an employee, you pay taxes on all your income. A business owner pays on his or her income after expenses. Business ownership offers many immediate tax savings in addition to long-term strategies that lower your taxes when you reinvest in or expand your business.

The Most Obvious Advantages

The most obvious tax benefit for business owners is the ability to deduct business expenses directly from their income, reducing their overall taxable income. The two most vital aspects of this benefit are understanding what constitutes a legitimate business expense and keeping meticulous records so you don't miss any deductions.

Entrepreneurs operating out of their homes can deduct certain costs associated with maintaining their home offices if they meet IRS guidelines. These could include a portion of their rent or mortgage, utilities, and insurance proportional to the amount of space dedicated to business operations. Navigating the specific requirements to qualify for the home office deduction can optimize tax savings for home-based businesses.

Even an entrepreneur with a business location outside their home can usually take advantage of this deduction by doing all their administrative work from a home office. This can significantly increase their deductions for automobile expenses by turning otherwise non-deductible commuting into a business expense.

Self-employed individuals can deduct 100 percent of their health insurance premiums for themselves, their spouses, and their dependents directly from their taxable income. Given the high cost of health insurance, this deduction can offer significant savings, making it a critical tax advantage for business owners without access to employer-sponsored health plans.

Business ownership also opens avenues for retirement savings with tax advantages through vehicles like SEP IRAs,

SIMPLE IRAs, solo 401(k)s, and even pension plans. Contributions to these plans are often tax-deductible, reducing taxable income while simultaneously building a retirement nest egg. The higher contribution limits associated with some of these plans compared to traditional retirement accounts offer an additional benefit.

Various tax credits are available to businesses that contribute to society through specific activities. This includes hiring employees from designated target groups, investing in research and development, or implementing environmentally friendly practices. Unlike deductions, which reduce taxable income, credits reduce tax liability dollar-for-dollar, making them incredibly valuable for eligible businesses.

Various tax credits are available to businesses that contribute to society through specific activities.

Business owners can also deduct the cost of capital expenditures, such as equipment and vehicles, either over the life of the asset or immediately under Section 179 and/or bonus depreciation provisions. These deductions eliminate the tax on income reinvested in the business. In the early years, these deductions can even create a tax loss that can be used to offset income from other sources, such as their spouse's employment or business income.

Businesses that operate at a loss in the initial years can generally use their losses to offset other income if they are a pass-through entity such as a partnership, sole proprietorship, or S corporation. These losses can also offset future profits (carryforward) when they are a C corporation, providing a financial cushion and cash flow relief as they grow and stabilize.

Navigating the tax benefits available to business owners requires strategic planning, good tax advisors, and meticulous record-keeping. By leveraging these tax advantages, entrepreneurs can significantly reduce their tax liabilities, improve cash flow, and reinvest in their businesses for accelerated growth and long-term success. Understanding and applying these fiscal strategies empowers business owners to optimize their operations financially, turning tax savings into an engine for business development and sustainability.

Transitioning from an Employee to an Entrepreneur Can Lead To Tax-Savvy Success

Transitioning from employee to entrepreneur opens a new world of tax-saving opportunities. While employees primarily rely on their W2 forms to manage their taxes, entrepreneurs have access to a broader spectrum of tax deductions and strategies that can lead to significant savings and, ultimately, tax-savvy success. This transition is not just about changing the way you work; it's about transforming how your finances, especially taxes, can be optimized for better financial health and business growth.

As an entrepreneur, the range of expenses that can potentially qualify as tax-deductible widens significantly. Unlike employees with limited tax-deductible work-related expenses, entrepreneurs can deduct a vast array of business expenses directly from their income, lowering their taxable income.

Business owners just have to follow these four simple tests to make their expenses deductible:

1. There must be a business purpose to the expense.

2. The expense must be ordinary, meaning typical to their business and in the amount spent.

3. The expense must be necessary, meaning it is either spent to increase profits or market share.

4. The expense must be properly documented. This means original receipts (or scanned receipts) and, in some cases, business meals and travel, as well as additional information justifying the expense.

Deductible expenses can include but are not limited to office supplies, marketing and advertising costs, business travel, business meals and home office deductions. Understanding and leveraging these deductions can substantially reduce your tax liability.

In the early stages of business, it's common to incur losses. While no one aims for losses, the silver lining for entrepreneurs is the ability to use these losses to offset other income on their tax returns, including investment or a spouse's income. This can result in a lower overall tax bill, providing some financial relief during the challenging initial phase of building a business. In many cases, the tax benefits of starting a business can outweigh the costs of starting a business. Check out all the details in chapter two of *The Win-Win Wealth Strategy* by Tom Wheelwright.

Entrepreneurs have more flexibility in choosing retirement plans, often with higher contribution limits than traditional employee plans. This allows for more substantial annual contributions and offers tax benefits through deferred taxation or non-taxed investment income. These plans can be critical components of an entrepreneur's tax strategy and retirement planning, offering both immediate tax benefits and long-term financial growth. Alternative investments for retirement, including owning the building you use for your business, can create additional tax benefits for a business owner. Transitioning to entrepreneurship brings the responsibility of covering self-employment taxes, including the employee and employer portion of Social Security and Medicare taxes. However, strategic business structuring and tax planning can mitigate these additional costs. For example, forming an S Corporation can allow entrepreneurs to pay themselves a reasonable salary, with any additional profits taken as distributions. While the salary is subject to social security taxes, the distributions are not subject to either social security or self-employment taxes. This strategy requires careful planning with the help of a qualified tax advisor who can help you stay in compliance with IRS rules and lead you to substantial tax savings.

Entrepreneurship requires a proactive approach to tax planning. Utilizing the services of a tax professional who understands business taxes can unveil strategies that minimize liabilities and maximize benefits. Tax planning becomes an integral part of financial decision-making, influencing when and how to make significant purchases, invest in the business, or take distributions. This level of strategic planning is seldom available to employees and can be a game-changer for entrepreneurs.

Entrepreneurs significantly enhance their financial standing by leveraging the broader range of tax deductions, understanding how to use business losses, making smart retirement contributions, and employing advanced tax strategies. This transition requires a shift in mindset—from seeing taxes as a mere obligation to viewing them as a strategic tool for building a successful and financially robust business.

The Importance of Tax Planning

Understanding the tax benefits accompanying business ownership is crucial for effective financial planning and decision-making. In the move from employee to entrepreneur, the focus on taxes expands to include optimizing the business's financial performance and leveraging tax advantages to support business growth and sustainability. This includes a strategic approach to categorizing expenses, making capital investments, and choosing a business structure that offers favorable tax treatment. Understanding the fundamentals of business taxation is pivotal for any entrepreneur looking to navigate the complexities of tax planning and compliance effectively.

A sole proprietorship is the simplest business structure. In this designation, the business is not legally distinct from the owner. The owner reports the business's profits and losses on their personal tax return using Schedule C. This structure offers simplicity in tax filing **A sole proprietorship is the simplest business structure.** but does not provide a separation between personal and business liabilities. Even a sole proprietor should have a separate bank account. For tax purposes, the business income is subject to self-employment taxes in addition to income tax.

Partnerships involve two or more individuals who share ownership of a business. Like sole proprietorships, partnerships are "pass-through" entities for tax purposes, meaning the business itself is not taxed. Instead, profits and losses are passed through to the partners, and each partner pays taxes on their share of the income. This portion can also be subject to self-employment taxes. Forming a partnership requires an agreement on the distribution of profits and losses, and partners must file an annual information return to report business income, deductions, and more.

Limited Liability Corporations (LLCs) offer flexibility in taxation. Owners (members) can choose how they are taxed: as a sole proprietorship, partnership, or corporation. This structure provides the asset protection of a corporation with the tax benefits of a pass-through entity. For single-member LLCs, the default taxation is that of a sole proprietorship, while multi-member LLCs are taxed as partnerships by default. LLCs can also elect to be taxed as S Corporations or C Corporations, potentially offering tax savings on self-employment taxes.

Corporations, including C corporations and S corporations, are considered legal entities separate from their owners. They offer asset protection and additional tax benefits. C Corporations are subject to corporate income tax and face potential double taxation—once at the corporate level on profits and again at the individual level on dividends distributed to shareholders. However, they can benefit from lower corporate tax rates that are unavailable to pass-through entities. Structured properly, a C corporation can also result in avoiding capital gains tax when the business is sold.

S Corporations, designed for businesses, avoid double taxation by passing profits and losses directly to shareholders, who then report this income on their personal tax returns. S Corporations are subject to strict eligibility requirements and have limitations on the number and type of shareholders. As mentioned previously, one of the primary tax benefits of an S Corporation is the ability to reduce employment taxes for the owner.

Selecting the right business structure is a critical decision that impacts tax obligations, asset protection, and the ability to attract investment. Factors to consider include the size and nature of the business, the plans for growth, and the level of acceptable personal risk. Consulting with tax professionals and legal advisors is crucial in making an informed choice that aligns with your business goals and maximizes tax advantages.

Selecting the right business structure is a critical decision that impacts tax obligations, asset protection, and the ability to attract investment.

A good tax strategy typically begins with an assessment of the best business structure. By carefully selecting the most appropriate legal structure for your business, you can optimize tax advantages, protect personal assets, and lay a solid foundation for financial success.

The Section 179 Deduction

The Section 179 Deduction is one of the key tax benefits available to business owners. This provision allows businesses to deduct the full purchase price of qualifying equipment and software purchased or financed during the tax year rather than depreciating the cost over several years. This stands out as a significant tax advantage, offering business owners an opportunity to maximize tax savings while investing in the growth of their businesses.

To qualify for the Section 179 deduction, the assets acquired must be used more than 50 percent of the time for business purposes. This can include machinery, equipment, computers used in the business, and any software readily available for purchase by the general public, subject to a non-exclusive license and not substantially modified. Certain improvements made to the interior portion of a non-residential building after the building is placed in service qualify for the Section 179 Deduction, as do certain heavy vehicles, such as trucks and SUVs, that meet specific weight criteria.

The Section 179 deduction is subject to annual dollar limits and a phase-out threshold, adjusted annually for inflation. For the tax year 2025, the maximum deduction limit is set at $1,250,000, and the phase-out threshold starts at $3,130,000 of total equipment purchases. This means the deduction begins to reduce dollar-for-dollar beyond this threshold, fully phasing out when equipment purchases exceed $4,380,000.

Businesses exceeding the phase-out threshold can still benefit from the deduction but must carefully calculate the allowable deduction amount. The Section 179 deduction cannot exceed the business's taxable income; however, any unused portion of the deduction can be carried over to the next tax year. If Section 179 isn't available, you may be able to take advantage of bonus depreciation instead.

To claim the Section 179 deduction, businesses must complete Part I of IRS Form 4562: Depreciation and Amortization and attach it to their tax return. The form requires detailed information about the property, including the cost, date of acquisition, and the business-related portion of use. Maintaining accurate records and receipts of all purchases is crucial to substantiating the deduction in case of an IRS audit.

Utilizing the Section 179 deduction effectively requires strategic planning, especially in terms of timing purchases to maximize tax benefits. For businesses anticipating significant income, making qualifying purchases before the end of the tax year can reduce taxable income and, thus, tax liability. Conversely, if a lower income year is expected, deferring purchases to offset higher income anticipated in future years might be advantageous.

Additionally, businesses should consider how the Section 179 deduction interacts with other tax provisions, such as bonus depreciation, to optimize overall tax savings. Combining these provisions often results in significant tax relief, further supporting business growth and investment. As tax laws and limits can change, it's advisable to consult with a tax professional to ensure compliance and optimal use of this valuable tax benefit.

Bonus Depreciation

In addition to Section 179 deductions, bonus depreciation serves as a potent tax-saving strategy, allowing businesses to immediately deduct a significant percentage of the purchase price of eligible assets. This provision is particularly beneficial for businesses making substantial investments in new or used property and equipment, allowing for the immediate deduction of a significant portion of the asset's cost.

Bonus depreciation allows businesses to deduct a specified percentage of the cost of eligible assets in the year they are placed in service, thus accelerating the recovery of their investment costs. To qualify, assets must be new or used tangible property with a recovery period of twenty years or less. This includes machinery, equipment, computers, software, and certain vehicles. Certain improvements to real property, such as landscaping and outdoor lighting, may also qualify.

Bonus depreciation allows businesses to deduct a specified percentage of the cost of eligible assets in the year they are placed in service.

The percentage of the cost that can be deducted has varied over the years due to changes in tax laws. It's crucial to consult current tax regulations or a tax professional to determine the exact percentage applicable in the current tax year. For 2025, a bonus depreciation of forty percent is allowed for certain assets acquired and placed in service by December 31.

To claim bonus depreciation, the asset must be used for business purposes, and the bonus depreciation amount is only applicable to the business use portion. You'll need documentation to support your deduction and use. Plus, you'll have to complete the appropriate sections of your tax return.

Bonus depreciation can be strategically used in conjunction with Section 179 deductions to maximize tax savings. While Section 179 allows for the expensing of assets up to a certain limit, bonus depreciation can be applied to amounts exceeding that limit or to assets not qualifying under Section 179. Businesses anticipating rapid growth can leverage bonus depreciation to invest in essential assets while minimizing their current tax liability. This strategic approach supports expansion and scaling efforts by improving cash flow through tax savings.

Like the Section 179 deduction, spreading out bonus depreciation over several years may be more beneficial in some cases. Business owners must understand that tax laws and provisions surrounding bonus depreciation are subject to change. As with all tax strategies, consultation with a tax professional is recommended to tailor the approach to the business's specific needs and circumstances.

In addition to the abovementioned strategies, entrepreneurs must consider long-term business goals and asset needs to take advantage of tax-efficient growth. A tax advisor, such as a CPA, who understands the intricacies of business taxation can provide tailored advice on maximizing tax advantages. Professional guidance is invaluable in navigating the complexities of tax planning.

The Section 179 deduction and bonus depreciation represent key tax advantages that can provide significant and transformative opportunities for business growth. Understanding and utilizing these tax benefits greatly influences a new business's financial health and expansion potential.

Even in the beginning stages of your entrepreneurial endeavors, carefully timed purchases, balancing tax benefits, and planning investments with immediate and long-term tax efficiency in mind can significantly enhance your business's financial foundation. This strategy underscores the importance of informed, proactive tax planning in the entrepreneurial journey, transforming potential tax liabilities into opportunities for investment and growth.

Case Studies

The transformative power of tax-saving strategies is best illustrated through real-life applications, where business owners across various industries have navigated the complexities of tax benefits to bolster their financial success.

One business specializing in technology solutions for local businesses capitalized on Section 179 deductions by investing in new computer systems and software. This strategic investment upgraded its operational capacity and allowed it to deduct the full purchase price of these assets in the same tax year, substantially reducing its taxable income. The company reinvested its realized savings from this tax strategy into marketing efforts, leading to increased brand visibility and customer acquisition.

A construction company, recognizing the benefits of bonus depreciation, expanded its fleet of vehicles and heavy machinery. By leveraging bonus depreciation, the company was able to deduct a significant portion of the investment cost in the first year, thus lowering its tax liability. This timely expansion enabled the company to take on larger projects and enter new markets, illustrating how tax benefits can support financial savings and strategic business growth.

A boutique retail store owner utilized Section 179 deductions and bonus depreciation when renovating their storefront and purchasing new inventory management software. By carefully planning these purchases and investments, the boutique minimized its taxable income while enhancing the shopping experience for its customers. The tax savings contributed to funding an online sales platform, diversifying the business's revenue streams, and increasing its resilience against market fluctuations.

An independent publishing company took advantage of Section 179 deductions by investing in new printing equipment and technology. This allowed the publisher to bring more printing processes in-house, reducing costs and improving turnaround times for client projects. The savings gained from this tax strategy facilitated the launch of a digital publishing division, broadening the company's market reach and revenue potential.

A growing restaurant chain strategically applied bonus depreciation in its expansion to new locations, significantly reducing its tax burden for the year. This approach supported the chain's aggressive growth strategy and maximized its financial resources. The additional capital was used to enhance the dining experience across all locations, directly contributing to increased customer satisfaction and loyalty.

By understanding and leveraging tax benefits such as Section 179 deductions and bonus depreciation, business owners can significantly reduce their tax liabilities, freeing up capital for reinvestment in areas that drive growth, innovation, and competitive advantage. The strategic use of tax advantages is a powerful tool in the entrepreneur's financial toolkit, demonstrating that with informed planning and execution, tax policy can be leveraged to support and accelerate business success.

Planning for Optimal Tax Advantages

Proactive tax planning is an essential component of strategic business management, ensuring entrepreneurs comply with tax laws and optimize their financial outcomes by leveraging available tax advantages. Effective planning involves a forward-looking approach to financial decisions, integrating tax considerations into the fabric of business strategy.

Staying informed about these changes is crucial for taking advantage of new tax benefits and avoiding pitfalls.

We recommend every entrepreneur schedule planning meetings with a tax professional at least four times each year to review performance and plan for tax-saving opportunities. These sessions should include reviewing asset purchases, potential investments, and any significant changes in the business that could impact tax liabilities.

Since tax laws are subject to change, staying informed about these changes is crucial for taking advantage of new tax benefits and avoiding pitfalls. A knowledgeable tax professional can provide updates on relevant tax law changes and advise on how these changes affect your business. A professional can also help plan the timing and nature of asset purchases with tax advantages in mind, such as Section 179 deductions and bonus depreciation. This involves assessing the need for equipment, technology, or vehicles in the context of current tax benefits and future business requirements.

Tax professionals can also offer expert advice tailored to your specific business circumstances, ensuring compliance with complex tax laws while identifying opportunities to minimize tax liabilities. Their expertise is particularly valuable in navigating the nuances of deductions, credits, and tax-efficient business structures.

Beyond annual tax planning, tax professionals can help develop a long-term tax strategy that aligns with business goals and growth plans. This strategy can include structuring the business to take advantage of favorable tax treatments, planning for succession or exit, and optimizing the tax implications of business expansion.

Regular reviews of your financial position and associated tax strategies allow for adjustments due to business growth, market changes, or shifts in tax laws. Continuous monitoring ensures that your tax planning remains aligned with your business objectives and the current tax environment.

The final element in successfully implementing these tax savings is maintaining meticulous records of all transactions, expenses, and investments. Good record-keeping is critical for compliance and provides a clear picture of your financial activities and their tax implications.

Caution

New entrepreneurs have responsibilities that they didn't have as an employee. This includes payroll reporting when you hire employees and 1099s for contractors. You will need to obtain a W-4 from your employees to tell you how much tax to withhold from their paychecks and file quarterly payroll reports. You will need to obtain a W-9 from any outside service providers and send them a 1099 at the end of the year. You may also have a separate tax return to file for your business entity.

As an employee, your employer would have withheld income taxes, so your only obligation was to file your tax return. As a business owner, you will need to pay quarterly estimated payments on Form 1040-ES. New entrepreneurs can get caught with unexpected tax bills when they file their tax returns, along with substantial penalties, if they have not paid quarterly estimated taxes on the income from their business and investments. This can be a rude awakening the first time you file your income tax return after a profitable year.

Key Takeaways

- **Entrepreneurship can give you significant tax savings.** The tax savings from your new business might even affect your tax burden from your W2 paycheck or your spouse's income.

- **Section 179 deductions and bonus depreciation create opportunities for substantial tax savings.**

- **Engaging with a tax professional makes for a great investment.** You have your specialty, and the tax professionals have theirs. By using the services of a CPA or other tax professional, you save yourself the time of learning the new tax laws every year.

- **Don't forget your new tax filing responsibilities.** As a business owner, you have responsibilities for new tax reporting, including reporting for your employees and outside service providers.

6

Crafting a Strategic Business Plan

well-conceived business plan plays a critical role in a
business's lifecycle. It serves as a cornerstone for securing
financing and guiding day-to-day operations. The plan
not only lays a solid foundation for your business's growth
but also appeals to lenders and investors, increasing the likelihood of obtaining the financial support needed for success.

The Importance of a Solid Business Plan

A comprehensive business plan is indispensable for several
reasons. First, it acts as a roadmap for your business, outlining your vision, mission, and the strategies you plan to
employ to achieve your goals. It provides a detailed overview
of your business model, market analysis, operational plans,
and financial projections, helping you navigate the complexities of starting and running a business.

Second, a well-crafted business plan is crucial in securing financing. Lenders and investors use your business plan to assess the viability and potential profitability of your business idea. It demonstrates to them that you have a thorough understanding of your market, a clear strategy for growth, and realistic financial projections. A persuasive business plan can be the difference between obtaining the necessary funding to propel your business forward and falling at the first hurdle due to a lack of financial support.

The indispensability of a solid business plan extends beyond its role as a mere document; it embodies the strategic blueprint and financial forecast that underpins the foundation of any successful business venture. This comprehensive guide serves multiple crucial purposes in the lifecycle of a business, each reinforcing its value and necessity.

A persuasive business plan can be the difference between obtaining the necessary funding to propel your business forward and falling at the first hurdle due to a lack of financial support.

At its core, a business plan acts as a strategic roadmap, meticulously detailing the journey from concept to execution. It encompasses the business's vision and mission, articulating the core values and the overarching goals that guide every decision and action. This roadmap delineates the strategies to be employed, outlining how the business intends to achieve its objectives through detailed operational plans. It provides clarity and direction, enabling entrepreneurs to anticipate challenges, allocate resources effectively, and steer the business toward its goals.

The Beginning of a Business Plan That Appeals to Lenders and Investors

Your business plan should open with a compelling *Executive Summary* that encapsulates the essence of your business venture. Begin by clearly articulating your business idea. You want your reader to instantly grasp what your business is about and the unique value it offers. Briefly describe your product or service and the problem it solves, and tell the world how it stands out from existing market offerings. Convey the essence of your business concept with clarity and enthusiasm.

Your Executive Summary will also include a summary of the market analysis for your business idea. Lenders and investors are keenly interested in the potential for their investment. Explain why there is a demand for your product or service, show market trends, and tell the reader how you plan to position your business to capitalize on the market share. You'll

Your Executive Summary will also include a summary of the market analysis for your business idea.

also want to list the size and characteristics of the customer segments in your target market using data and research to back up your numbers. Demonstrating a deep understanding of your industry and its dynamics will reassure financiers of the viability and the potential for your business to carve out a profitable niche within the market.

In addition, your Executive Summary should clearly articulate your business's competitive advantage. This could be a unique technology, an innovative business model, superior customer service, or exclusive partnerships. Detail how this advantage positions your business to succeed in the competitive landscape and sustain long-term growth. Convincingly presenting your competitive edge can significantly increase the appeal of your business plan to lenders and investors.

While detailed financial projections will appear later in your business plan, the Executive Summary should include a high-level financial overview. You should summarize key financial highlights, such as projected revenues, profit margins, and the anticipated return on investment. This snapshot gives lenders and investors a quick understanding of your business's financial health and profitability potential.

Conclude the executive summary by clearly stating the funding you require and how you plan to use it. Be specific about the amount needed, whether it's for capital expenditures, operational costs, or expansion efforts. Also, indicate the type of financing you're seeking, such as equity investment or a loan. Providing a clear call to action regarding your funding needs encourages potential financiers to consider how they might contribute to your business's success.

Crafting a business plan that captivates lenders and investors from the outset is paramount, and the Executive Summary serves as the critical entry point to this endeavor. This section contains more than an introduction. Your lenders and investors want to read a powerful story that conveys the core of your business proposition, compellingly and succinctly, and sets the stage for a compelling narrative that encourages further reading.

The Market Analysis

Though you gave a synopsis of the market analysis in the Executive Summary, as you move into the next section of your business plan, you'll want to expand on that and give your reader more details. A comprehensive market analysis is a cornerstone of any persuasive business plan. This part should provide evidence and insights to support your business proposition.

To show the reader you have a broad understanding of the industry landscape, you should provide an overview, including the industry's size, growth rate, and key trends. This macro perspective should highlight the industry's health and trajectory, indicating whether it's expanding, stable, or declining. Discuss any technological, regulatory, or economic factors that could impact the industry, providing a context for the opportunities and challenges your business might face.

Next, you'll narrow the focus of your discussion to your specific target market within the larger industry. Define your target customers by demographic, geographic, psychographic, and behavioral characteristics. Explain why you've chosen this segment and reiterate the size of this market opportunity. Detailed segmentation demonstrates that you understand who your customers are, what they need, and how to reach them, increasing confidence in your business's ability to attract and retain a solid customer base.

Your market includes your target audience's needs, preferences, and pain points. What are customers looking for? What gaps exist in the current market offerings? How does your product or service meet these needs more effectively than competitors? Presenting qualitative and quantitative data from market research, surveys, and focus groups can provide compelling evidence of customer demand.

Your market includes your target audience's needs, preferences, and pain points.

The market analysis section of your business plan also includes describing the competitive landscape. Who are the key players in your focused market? What are their market positions—their strengths and weaknesses? Discuss how your business differentiates itself from these competitors through better quality, innovation, pricing strategies, customer service, or technology. This analysis should showcase your understanding of the competition and highlight your unique value proposition and how it positions you to capture market share. Next, estimate the market share you aim to capture and project how this might grow over time. Base these projections on your competitive advantages, marketing strategies, and the scalability of your business model. Illustrating your business's growth potential within the market can significantly boost lenders' and investors' confidence in your venture.

Use this section to acknowledge potential market risks, such as emerging competitors, changes in consumer behavior, or regulatory developments. Present a clear plan for mitigating these risks to show investors your foresight and preparedness, further solidifying the credibility of your business plan.

The market analysis section of your business plan should blend data-driven insights with a clear narrative that communicates your deep understanding of market dynamics and your strategic approach to gaining a competitive edge. Demonstrating comprehensive market knowledge and a clear strategy for capturing market share will significantly enhance your business plan's appeal, making a compelling case for investment.

Include an Operational Plan

Investors want to know how your business will function on a day-to-day basis. Clarity in this area ensures the business is well-equipped to manage its operations and deliver products and services efficiently. Your operational plan will start by identifying your potential location and facilities.

- Why did you choose that location?
- What are the benefits?
- Does it have adequate customer access?
- What are the logistical advantages?

In that same vein, describe the facilities your business requires, including retail spaces, offices, warehouses, or manufacturing plants. Discuss the size, layout, and features of these facilities that will enable your business to operate efficiently. If you're leasing, mention the terms and how they align with your business needs. For an online business, explain how your digital presence will be established and maintained.

The operational part of your business plan will include the technology infrastructure that will support your business. Discuss your point-of-sale systems, inventory management software, customer relationship management (CRM) platform, and any industry-specific technologies you will need. Explain how these technologies will enhance operational efficiency, customer service, and data management.

Equipment also falls under the category of operating plans. List the critical equipment your business will use, whether for manufacturing, service delivery, or office operations. Include information on the acquisition of this equipment, whether you intend to purchase or lease, and how it fits into your operational processes.

Your investors will also want to know how you plan to get the job done. Will you have a workforce to back you up? Identify the roles and number of employees needed to operate your business effectively. Describe the skills and experience required for each role and your strategy for recruiting, hiring, and training staff.

Detail your business's management structure, including key management roles and responsibilities. This information should convey how your team's expertise and leadership will drive the business toward achieving its goals.

Describe the core operational processes that will drive your business, from production and inventory management to customer service and fulfillment. Outline how these processes will be managed and optimized for efficiency.

Part of operations is managing risk and compliance standards. Address relevant industry regulations, health and safety standards, and employment laws. Then, discuss how you will meet the criteria. Detail the measures you have in place to ensure ongoing compliance. You'll also want to discuss the operational risks your business could potentially face, such as supply chain disruptions or equipment failures. This section should include the strategies you have developed to mitigate these risks.

Finally, tell the reader how your operational plan will adapt to support future growth. This could include plans for expanding your facilities, scaling up production, or growing your workforce. Demonstrating scalability reassures lenders and investors of your business's potential for long-term success.

A well-thought-out operational plan is will demonstrate to lenders and investors that you have a practical and detailed strategy for running your business. By providing comprehensive information on these items, you effectively communicate your readiness to execute your business plan.

This detailed blueprint section of your business plan demonstrates how your business intends to achieve its goals and objectives through its daily function. It also provides lenders and investors with a clear vision of how your business operates.

Tell Investors About Your Marketing and Sales Strategy

Lenders and investors need to know you have a clear plan for generating revenue. Without the ability to turn a profit, the financiers will move on to something more lucrative. Begin by briefly reviewing your target market segments as well as their needs, preferences, and pain points. Though you touched on this briefly in a previous section, the truth is you can't have a market and sales strategy without a target audience. Show the reader that you understand how foundational your target audience is in tailoring your marketing and sales efforts effectively.

Outline your advertising strategy. Detail any promotional tactics. Explain how you will use the strategies.

Your marketing and sales strategy should also include ways to attract and retain customers. Describe how you plan to position your brand in the market. This includes your brand messaging, values, and unique value proposition that differentiates your business from competitors. A strong brand identity is crucial for resonating with your target audience and fostering loyalty.

Outline your advertising strategy, including the channels and mediums you will use to reach your target market, such as online advertising, social media, print media, or television. Detail any promotional tactics, such as discounts, loyalty programs, or special events, designed to attract new customers and engage existing ones. Explain how you will use content marketing and digital marketing strategies, including SEO, email marketing, content creation, and social media engagement, to attract and retain customers. Digital marketing is essential for reaching customers in today's market, offering both broad reach and targeted engagement.

Fifty years ago, almost all marketing was done through television, radio, and word of mouth, and sales were processed by mail order or, more commonly, face-to-face. Today, we have more sales channels than ever before. This part of your business plan should specify the sales channels through which your products or services will be sold, such as direct in-person sales, online sales, retail partnerships, or wholesale. Each channel should be chosen based on its effectiveness in reaching your target market and aligned with your overall business model.

Your business plan should discuss the sales processes and techniques you and your team will use to convert leads into customers. This may include sales funnel strategies, customer relationship management practices, and after-sales service policies to ensure customer satisfaction and repeat business. For example, investors will want to see a comprehensive overview of your pricing strategy. How does your model align with market expectations? What is its competitive positioning, and how does it work with your cost structure? Your pricing strategy should reflect the value provided to customers while supporting your revenue and profitability goals.

Your company's public relations (PR) strategy will become an important part of your business plan. How will you manage media relations, press releases, and events to build brand awareness and credibility? Your PR strategy includes your plans for community involvement and social responsibility initiatives you plan to implement that can enhance your brand's reputation and foster customer loyalty.

Finally, tell your reader how you plan to monitor and evaluate success. Begin by defining clear, measurable objectives for different aspects of your business. These could be financial goals, customer satisfaction targets, production levels, or marketing reach, among others. Then, establish benchmarks based on industry standards, past performance, or competitive analysis. These benchmarks serve as a reference point against which you can measure your current performance.

You also need to identify Key Performance Indicators (KPIs) that will measure the effectiveness of your marketing and sales strategies. You want to choose KPIs that are directly relevant to your business goals. For instance, if increasing customer retention is a goal, a relevant KPI could be the customer retention rate. Ensure a balanced set of KPIs covering various aspects of your business, including financial performance, customer engagement, operational efficiency, and employee satisfaction, and ensure they are easy to understand and measure. Overly complex indicators might lead to confusion and misinterpretation of data.

A robust marketing and sales strategy is essential for any business plan. It is the engine that drives revenue generation and customer engagement. The strategy should articulate a comprehensive approach to attracting and retaining customers through effective marketing and sales tactics and convincingly illustrate your business's potential for success in the competitive marketplace.

Include Detailed Financial Projections

A good business plan details financial projections for at least three to five years. It includes a projected profit and loss statement with detailed revenue and expense projections. Revenue projections break down income sources such as product sales, service fees, or other revenue streams based on your market analysis, sales strategy, and pricing model, providing a realistic estimate of how much money the business expects to generate over time. You'll also need to figure your gross margin by calculating the cost of goods sold (COGS), which includes direct materials, labor, and other direct costs, and subtract it from your revenue.

Expense projections outline all expected operating expenses, including marketing and advertising costs, salaries and wages, rent and utilities, insurance, and administrative costs. When you subtract your operating expenses from your gross margin, you'll have your bottom line, also known as net profit, showing the potential profitability of the business after all costs have been accounted for.

Financial projections also include cash flow projections—a detailed monthly or quarterly report of cash inflows and outflows. These numbers will highlight times the business expects to receive payments from customers and when expenses are due. This projection is vital for understanding the business's liquidity and ability to cover short-term liabilities. You can use cash flow projections to identify periods of tight liquidity and plan for working capital needs. This may involve securing lines of credit or other financing options to ensure the business can operate smoothly without cash flow interruptions. Include a break-even analysis to show when the business expects to become profitable on a cash flow basis. This analysis reassures lenders and investors of the business's sustainability and financial health.

Financial projections are vital for understanding the business's liquidity and ability to cover short-term liabilities.

This section of your business plan will also include a balance sheet listing expected assets, such as cash, inventory, and equipment; liabilities, like loans and accounts payable;

and business equity. The balance sheet provides a snapshot of the business's financial position at different points in the future, offering insight into its financial stability and growth potential.

As you finish your financial projections, clearly state the assumptions used to reach your conclusions, including growth rates, pricing strategies, market penetration rates, and cost estimates. These assumptions should be realistic and justifiable based on your market analysis and operational plans. Consider including a sensitivity analysis to show how changes in key assumptions could impact financial projections. This demonstrates to lenders and investors that you have considered various scenarios and are prepared for potential changes in the business environment.

Financial projections are a critical element of any business plan, offering a quantifiable outlook on your venture's anticipated financial performance. By providing comprehensive financial projections, you equip lenders and investors with the information needed to make informed decisions about your business. Moreover, these projections serve as a valuable roadmap for you as a business owner. They can help guide your financial planning, resource allocation, and strategic decision-making as you strive to achieve your business objectives.

Risk Analysis

Include a risk analysis that identifies potential challenges your business may face and the strategies you will employ to mitigate them. Demonstrating that you have considered the risks and have plans in place to address them can significantly increase confidence among potential financiers.

You'll need to address several risk categories. Begin by analyzing and detailing risks related to market demand fluctuations, competitive pressures, or changes in consumer preferences. Understanding the dynamics of your market and potential shifts can help you formulate strategies to remain relevant and competitive. Next, identify risks that could impact your day-to-day operations, such as supply chain disruptions, key personnel turnover, or technology failures. Outline how operational efficiencies and contingencies are designed to safeguard against these risks.

Third, address financial challenges your business might face, including cash flow shortages, unexpected expenses, or difficulties in securing financing. Explain the financial management practices and controls you have in place to monitor and manage financial health. Finally, outline the legal and regulatory risks your business might face. Consider potential changes in laws, regulations, or policies. Tell the reader how you plan to stay informed and compliant with relevant legal requirements to mitigate legal and regulatory risks.

Diversification helps mitigate risks associated with market volatility and supply disruptions.

In addition to the mitigation strategies you described for each of the risk categories, you might include plans on how to implement diversification. Dependence on a single revenue source or supplier can increase your risk. Diversification helps mitigate risks associated with market volatility and supply disruptions. Having a robust financial plan can also reduce risk. In your business plan, you can highlight the importance of conservative financial planning, maintaining adequate cash reserves, and establishing lines of credit to manage financial risks effectively. This includes regular financial analysis to anticipate and address cash flow challenges proactively.

Implementing technology and security measures rises to the top of risk management in today's electronic climate. Detail the use of advanced technology and security measures to protect against operational disruptions, data breaches, and cyber threats. Explain how investing in technology infrastructure and cybersecurity can safeguard your operations and sensitive information.

You'll also want to outline your approach to managing regulatory and legal risks. Give your reader a comprehensive look at your compliance programs. This could involve regular legal audits, employee training on legal and regulatory requirements, and engaging with legal advisors. Finally, include your monitoring process to quickly identify risks and review your mitigation strategies. This should include setting up risk management teams or committees, employing risk assessment tools, and conducting regular risk reviews to adapt to new threats and changes in the business environment.

Including a thorough risk analysis and presenting clear mitigation strategies in your business plan underscores your commitment to responsible business management. It shows potential financiers that you are aware of the challenges your business may face and are prepared to address them effectively. This level of preparedness can significantly enhance their confidence in your business's ability to navigate uncertainties and sustain growth over the long term. By demonstrating strategic foresight in risk management, you strengthen your case for investment, positioning your business as a calculated and manageable risk for lenders and investors.

One major goal of your business plan is to secure financing. The importance of this aspect cannot be overstated. Lenders and investors critically evaluate the business plan to assess the risk and potential return on their investment. A well-crafted business plan can significantly influence their decision to provide funding.

Key Takeaways

- **The goal of a business plan is to create a road-map for the entrepreneur and instill confidence in lenders and investors.**

- **A well-crafted business plan includes several vital components.**

    o   An Executive Summary
    o   A Market Analysis
    o   An Operational Plan
    o   A Marketing and Sales Plan
    o   Financial Projections
    o   A Risk Analysis

- **The creation of a strategic business plan is not a mere formality.** It is a crucial step in the journey toward business success. It demands thorough research, careful analysis, and strategic foresight. A tailored plan that appeals to the discerning eyes of lenders and investors lays the foundation for a venture that is not only financially viable but also primed for long-term growth and success in the competitive business arena.

7

Understanding the Financial Landscape

Navigating the financial landscape and the various funding avenues can be daunting for prospective entrepreneurs. The financial ecosystem offers a range of financing solutions, each with unique characteristics, advantages, and drawbacks. Fortunately, your well-crafted business plan has all the components lenders and investors need to make decisions. Your next step will be understanding the plethora of financing options, each tailored to meet different needs, stages of business development, and financial profiles. This will allow you to make informed decisions that align with your business objectives and financial capacity.

Loans Partially Guaranteed by the Small Business Administration

Though the Small Business Administration (SBA) does not directly lend money to businesses, it does guarantee a portion of the loans made by participating lenders (up to 85 percent for loans under $150,000 and up to 75 percent for loans over $150,000). This guarantee reduces the risk to the lender in case of default, making them more willing to lend to businesses that might not qualify for conventional loans due to higher risk factors or lack of collateral. There are a variety of loan programs designed to assist businesses in obtaining the funding they need to flourish through the SBA. SBA loans are particularly attractive due to their relatively favorable terms, which often include lower down payments, competitive interest rates, and longer repayment terms than those typically offered by conventional loans.

The 7(a) Loan Program is the most common and flexible SBA loan, offering financial assistance for a wide range of business purposes, including working capital, refinancing existing debt, and purchasing real estate, equipment, or inventory. Specifically designed for purchasing major fixed assets, such as land, buildings, and machinery, that promote business growth and job creation, the 504 Loan Program features long-term, fixed-rate financing for major fixed assets. The SBA also has a Microloan Program that targets certain types of businesses and not-for-profit childcare centers that need small-scale funding of up to $50,000 to start up or expand. The average Microloan is about $13,000

To qualify for an SBA guaranteed loan, your business must fall into the SBA small business standards, operate for-profit in the United States, and have reasonable invested equity. The application process involves detailed documentation, including business and personal financial statements, income tax returns, business licenses, and a solid business plan. The process can be more involved than the conventional loan application, but the potential benefits often make it well worth the effort.

Conventional Financing

Conventional loans offered by banks, credit unions, and other financial institutions represent a more traditional route to business financing. Unlike SBA loans, conventional loans do not carry a government guarantee, which generally translates to stricter eligibility criteria, including higher credit score requirements and often the need for substantial collateral. The terms of conventional loans, including interest rates and repayment periods, can vary widely based on the lender's policies and the borrower's creditworthiness.

One of the primary considerations for conventional financing is the applicant's credit score. A strong credit score signals lenders that the borrower has a history of managing credit responsibility, allowing the institution to mitigate their risk. Be sure to monitor and improve your credit score to increase your chances of loan approval.

One of the primary considerations for conventional financing is the applicant's credit score.

Conventional loans also generally require collateral to secure the loan. This can include business assets, real estate, equipment, or other valuable assets. New businesses may find it more challenging to qualify for conventional financing due to the lack of operational history and proven revenue streams. Lenders look at new ventures as higher-risk investments, so personal credit scores and assets play a more significant role in the approval process.

Alternative Funding Options

Beyond SBA and conventional loans, entrepreneurs have access to a variety of alternative funding sources, each with unique benefits and considerations. Some of these sources also come with valuable business expertise and networking opportunities. Still, they require a more careful evaluation of their alignment with your business's growth stage, industry, and financial strategy.

High-growth startups with significant market potential might consider Venture Capital funding. In this model, investors finance ventures in exchange for a stake in the company. While offering substantial funding and valuable mentorship, entrepreneurs give up a portion of ownership and, in some cases, control. These lenders generally look for a strong team, a scalable business model, and significant market potential, and the field can be highly competitive.

Similar to venture capitalists, Angel Investors provide capital in exchange for equity. These affluent investors are often retired entrepreneurs or executives who want to use their experience and networks to mentor and groom new business endeavors. Typically, these individuals may offer more favorable terms and can provide valuable insights.

Crowdfunding platforms like Kickstarter, Indiegogo, and GoFundMe allow businesses to raise small amounts of money from a large number of people, often in exchange for early access to products or other rewards. This can be an excellent way to gauge interest in a product or service before full-scale production begins. Crowdfunding generally requires compelling storytelling and robust promotion to succeed. While successful campaigns can provide the capital you need, the funding model requires significant effort. Poorly executed crowdfunding can damage your brand.

Peer-to-peer lending uses online platforms to match borrowers with individual lenders to offer an alternative to traditional bank loans. P2P lending often provides quick turnaround, as well as more competitive interest rates, accessible loan terms, and flexible lending criteria

Platforms like SeedInvest and WeFunder facilitate Equity Crowdfunding transactions, enabling businesses to raise capital directly from a broad audience of investors who fund startups in return for equity. The regulatory framework offers transparency and protection and opens access to a larger pool of investors. On the other hand, it also involves sharing ownership and adhering to specific regulatory requirements.

Understanding the financial ecosystem to secure the right type of funding is a critical step in business development. Each financing option carries its own set of characteristics, advantages, and potential drawbacks. By thoroughly researching these options, entrepreneurs can strategically select the financing solution that best supports their business's needs, growth potential, and financial health, laying a solid foundation for long-term success.

Creditworthiness and Financial Health

In addition to the components you include in your business plan—initial set-up costs, operational expenses, cash flow needs, contingency funds, scalability and growth, and revenue predictions—your personal and business credit scores can significantly impact your ability to secure financing. Building and maintaining strong credit is essential, as is managing existing debt and ensuring your financial statements accurately reflect your business's health.

Lenders often examine your personal and business credit scores to assess the risk associated with lending to you. While personal credit scores are crucial for new entrepreneurs without an established business credit history, business credit scores become increasingly important as your venture grows.

The first step in establishing and maintaining strong credit involves making regular, on-time payments for all credit obligations. Your payment history makes a difference from credit cards to loans and vendor accounts.

Properly managing debt is also crucial for maintaining financial health and demonstrating creditworthiness. This includes keeping your balances well below your credit limits and creating a plan to manage and prioritize debt repayment. Often, focusing on high-interest or high-balance debts that can quickly erode your financial stability helps keep your debt under control. Some entrepreneurs leverage the power of refinancing to secure lower interest rates or more favorable terms. You'll also want to keep an eye on your debt-to-income ratio, which compares the amount you owe each month to your income. A lower ratio tells lenders you're more likely to manage additional debt payments effectively.

You'll also want to limit the number of hard inquiries to credit reporting agencies for a period of time before you apply for a loan. Each time you apply for credit, including loans and credit cards, a hard inquiry is made, which can lower your credit score.

Establishing a clear separation between personal and business finances is vital.

Regularly reviewing your credit reports for any inaccuracies or fraudulent activities can help eliminate surprises when you apply for your funding. Dispute any errors you find with the credit bureaus, as these can negatively impact your score.

Establishing a clear separation between personal and business finances is vital. This separation helps build your business credit profile and can protect your personal credit from business-related issues. The health of your business is often judged by the accuracy and clarity of your financial statements.

Balance sheets, income statements, and cash flow statements must be accurate, up-to-date, and reflect your business's financial situation. These documents are crucial for lenders assessing your business's viability and financial stability. Engaging with accounting professionals to review or audit these statements, especially when seeking significant financing, can increase your transparency, add a level of credibility to your financial reporting, and provide you with insights into areas for improvement.

Collateral and Guarantees

Many lenders require you to offer tangible or intangible assets as security against your loan. In the event of default, the lender has the right to seize the collateral to recoup the loan amount. Collateral can include real estate, equipment, inventory, accounts receivable, and even intellectual property.

When considering which assets to offer, you'll want to keep potential future needs for collateral in mind. Additionally, maintaining a diversified portfolio of both liquid and fixed assets can provide flexibility in securing loans while protecting critical business operations.

Lenders will assess the value of the proposed collateral, consider its current market value, and determine how easily it can be liquidated. Entrepreneurs need to be realistic about the value of their assets and prepared to provide documentation or appraisals to substantiate their worth. Using assets as collateral carries inherent risks. If the business fails to repay the loan, you risk losing these assets. Entrepreneurs must carefully evaluate which assets to offer as collateral, considering both the necessity of the loan and the criticality of the assets to the business's operations.

> **Providing a personal guarantee exposes the entrepreneur's personal assets to risk.**

Some financial institutions will lend money based on a personal guarantee, a signed commitment from the business owner to be personally responsible for the loan if the business cannot repay it. This may involve pledging personal assets as collateral, such as a home or personal savings. Providing a personal guarantee exposes the entrepreneur's personal assets to risk. It also blurs the line between personal and business finances, meaning that the entrepreneur's financial health is directly tied to the success of the business.

Before agreeing to a personal guarantee, entrepreneurs should thoroughly understand the terms and consider the potential impact on their personal financial situation. It's often advisable to consult with a legal or financial advisor to fully grasp the implications and explore possible limitations or caps on the guarantee to mitigate personal risk.

Understanding and carefully managing the requirements for collateral and personal guarantees are crucial for making informed financing decisions. These aspects of loan agreements impact the immediate ability to secure funding and have long-term implications for both the business and the entrepreneur's financial health. By thoughtfully evaluating which assets to use as collateral and considering the implications of personal guarantees, entrepreneurs can navigate the complexities of financing while safeguarding their assets and financial future.

Interest Rates and Repayment Terms

Interest rates and repayment terms are pivotal factors that directly impact the overall cost of borrowing and the financial sustainability of your business. Interest rates can be either fixed or variable. As you might imagine, fixed rates remain constant over the life of the loan, while variable rates fluctuate based on market conditions. Fixed rates offer predictability in budgeting and financial planning, while variable rates may initially be lower but carry the risk of increasing over time.

Interest rates can also vary significantly between lenders and loan products. Shop around and compare rates, considering the APR (Annual Percentage Rate), which includes not just the interest rate but any other fees associated with the loan. This comprehensive comparison ensures you're aware of the total cost of borrowing.

Repayment terms affect both your monthly payment and the total interest you'll pay over the life of the loan. Longer terms can lower your monthly payments but result in higher overall interest costs, while shorter terms increase monthly payments but decrease total interest.

You'll also want to understand the loan's amortization schedule. This outlines how payments are applied to principal and interest over time, and your awareness can help you assess the impact of repayment terms on your finances. Typically, a larger portion of your payment goes toward interest, with the balance shifting toward the principal over time.

Borrowers need to be aware of any penalties set up for early repayment.

Borrowers need to be aware of any penalties set up for early repayment. Clarifying the existence and terms of any prepayment penalties is important when evaluating loan options, especially if you anticipate improved cash flow or profitability that could allow for early debt retirement.

To understand the true financial impact of a loan, you'll want to calculate the total cost of borrowing. Add in all the interest and fees over the life of the loan, including the pre-payment penalty, if any. You can use this calculation in your strategic financial planning and growth projections.

Before making the final decision on the best financing option for their business, entrepreneurs should negotiate the terms, including interest, the length of the loan, collateral, and guarantees. Lenders may be willing to accept a portion of the loan amount as secured, reduce the scope of personal guarantees, or agree to more favorable conditions.

Key Takeaways

- **Carefully consider the best financing options for your business.** With the variety of options available, you'll need to decide which one fits your situation best:
  - o SBA Secured Loan
  - o Conventional Financing
  - o Alternative Financing

- **Be highly aware of your personal and business credit scores** and take the steps necessary to build those scores and increase your financial health.

- **Assess your assets to determine which will be the best use for collateral.**

8

Navigating SBA Financing

Small Business Administration (SBA) loans can be one of the biggest mysteries for people embarking on the journey from employee to entrepreneur. They also stand out as a valuable resource for new business owners. These loans are designed to provide accessible financing options to businesses that might not qualify for traditional bank loans.

What Defines a Small Business?

Understanding who qualifies for an SBA loan is the first step in tapping into this resource. Business size is crucial for determining eligibility for various SBA loan programs. The SBA uses one of two primary criteria to define a small business: number of employees or annual receipts. The limits vary depending on the business's North American Industry Classification System (NAICS) class. For example, the maximum number of employees a company can have and still be considered small by the SBA ranges from as few as 100 employees in some wholesale merchant categories and up to 1,500 employees in manufacturing-type industries.

The SBA uses annual gross receipts to determine a business's size in retail stores, agriculture, and construction sectors. The threshold typically ranges from $1 million to over $40 million and is calculated based on a three-year rolling average of sales and revenue.

Only businesses that meet these size standards qualify for most SBA loan programs. As mentioned previously, these programs offer benefits like lower down payments, more favorable terms, and easier qualification criteria than conventional loans.

Meeting SBA size standards goes beyond mere financing. Businesses that qualify under SBA guidelines might also be eligible for government contracting opportunities reserved for businesses, including set-asides and preferential treatment in bidding processes. Additionally, businesses that fit these size criteria can access other SBA resources, including business grants, training, and counseling services.

You can use the tables on the SBA website to determine whether your business meets the SBA's size standards. First, you'll need to identify your industry NAICS code; then, you can assess your eligibility according to the current relevant standard. Finally, you'll have to consider the aggregation rules. If your business is affiliated with other entities, their employees or receipts may need to be included in your total.

Other Requirements

The SBA provides financial assistance primarily to for-profit businesses. This means that the primary goal of the business should be to generate income above its expenses, leading to profitability. Non-profit organizations, even though they play crucial roles in their communities, are generally not eligible for most types of SBA loan programs because they do not operate with the intention to make a profit.

Businesses applying for SBA loans must demonstrate their for-profit status through organizational structure and financial documentation. This typically includes registration as a corporation, partnership, sole proprietorship, or limited liability company (LLC) that operates for profit. Financial records should clearly reflect a motive to generate income.

To qualify for an SBA loan, a business must be based and operating in the United States or its territories and provide proof of operation within eligible locations. This could include business licenses, tax records, and incorporation documents that specify the company's primary operations and management location. This criterion ensures that the benefits of SBA programs support the domestic economy, contributing to economic growth and job creation within the U.S.

By restricting eligibility to for-profit businesses operating within the U.S. and its territories, the SBA ensures that its resources are invested in entities that contribute directly to the American economy. This approach aims to foster domestic business growth, support job creation, and stimulate regional economic development. For-profit enterprises will likely repay debts and continue contributing economically through business activities and tax payments. This makes them viable candidates for government-backed loans, ensuring a cycle of reinvestment and return on public funds.

The SBA has a variety of loan programs, and each has unique guidelines and prerequisites tailored to support different business needs and objectives. The 7(a) Loan Program is the most general and can be used for almost any business need, while the 504 Loan Program is perfect for purchasing real estate or heavy equipment. Microloan programs are designed to assist with smaller funding needs. Start by determining which program best fits your business goals and whether or not you meet the criteria.

Each SBA loan program also has specific loan limits and restrictions on how the loan funds can be used and requires specific forms. Some also request additional documents, so it's essential to understand the program that best fits your needs so you can gather all necessary paperwork ahead of time.

The SBA offers tools to assist you, including the Lender Match tool, which helps you find lenders that offer the specific SBA loan you are interested in. This can also provide insights into specific lender requirements, which may vary slightly from the standard SBA guidelines.

Owner's Equity

The Small Business Administration also considers owner equity an essential criterion for loan eligibility. This requirement serves as a testament to the owner's dedication and belief in their business, reassuring lenders of the venture's seriousness and potential viability.

The most straightforward form of owner's equity is his or her direct financial investment into the business. This can include initial capital to start the business, personal funds used for operating expenses, or reinvestment of profits back into the business. Demonstrating that you have "skin in the game" financially shows lenders that you are willing to assume risk alongside them, which is a strong indicator of your commitment. The time, effort, and resources an owner invests in their business are equally significant.

Lenders and the SBA also consider the work the business owner puts into developing the business concept, creating products or services, and managing daily operations. For the SBA and potential lenders, a substantial investment of time can sometimes be as persuasive as a monetary investment, particularly in startups or businesses in their early stages, where financial data might be limited.

Demonstrating that you have "skin in the game" financially shows lenders that you are willing to assume risk alongside them.

By requiring owners to invest their own resources into their business, lenders ensure that owners are motivated to see the business succeed. Owners are less likely to walk away from a business in which they have substantial personal investments.

Owner's equity is also a key indicator of a business's financial health and gives it an enhanced creditworthiness. A healthy level of owner's equity can boost the business's balance sheet, making it more attractive to lenders. It reduces the debt-to-equity ratio, a critical factor during the loan approval process, and shows lenders the entrepreneur has more at stake both financially and personally, which can lead to more prudent financial management.

You'll want to have financial statements or time logs—or both—to reflect the capital considerations or non-monetary efforts you personally invested into your business. Legal documents such as incorporation papers or partnership agreements that specify the owner's investment can also be used to demonstrate equity. These documents often outline the initial contributions required from each of the business's partners or shareholders.

Repayment Ability

The requirement to demonstrate repayment ability is a critical aspect of securing any type of business loan. In addition to the cash flow analysis you create for your business plan, you'll want to know your Debt Service Coverage Ratio (DSCR). This ratio compares the business's net operating income to its total debt service obligations and the principal and interest payments due within a year. A DSCR of greater than one indicates that the business generates sufficient cash flow to cover its debt obligations.

Lenders will also want to see historical financial statements showing profitability and positive cash flow, as well as pro-forma financial statements. These forward-looking projections estimate expected cash inflows and outflows.

Demonstrating how your business will manage under various economic or business scenarios can further strengthen your case. This includes stress testing your cash flow projections against possible downturns or disruptions in the market. Showing you have contingency plans to handle adverse conditions can reassure lenders about your preparedness and financial resilience.

While demonstrating repayment ability primarily concerns cash flow, collateral or personal guarantees can also support it. These offer additional security to the lender and can be particularly persuasive if cash flow projections are less certain.

Highlighting the experience and track record of the management team can also support your repayment ability claims. Experienced leaders who have successfully navigated financial challenges or grown businesses in the past provide confidence that they can manage loan obligations effectively.

Application Process

The SBA loan application process can be daunting. Understanding each step can demystify it and increase your chances of success.

Stage One: Preparation

Gather the necessary documents, including detailed business plans, financial statements, projections, and the last three years' tax returns. These documents should convincingly demonstrate the viability and financial health of your business.

Prepare for your loan application using the SBA's resources, including counselors in the district offices and resource partners like SCORE, Women's Business Centers, and Small Business Development Centers. These resources can offer guidance, help you understand loan requirements, and even assist in preparing your loan application. You might also consider consulting with financial advisors or loan specialists with SBA loan experience. They can offer insights into the application process and tips on increasing your chances of approval.

Prepare for your loan application using the SBA's resources.

We also recommend creating a checklist of all required steps and documents based on the requirements of the SBA loan program. Establish a timeline for completing each step, especially if you need to gather financial records or obtain appraisals.

The preparation stage of applying for a loan, particularly an SBA loan, is critical in setting the foundation for a successful application. Well-prepared documentation can significantly smooth the loan application process, increase credibility, and improve your chances of securing the needed financing.

Stage Two: Find a Lender

Banks and financial institutions participate in SBA programs, but their terms and interests may vary. Finding the right lender is a crucial step in securing an SBA loan. Not all lenders offer the same level of experience with SBA programs. Consider their experience not just with SBA loans but also within your specific industry. Lenders with industry expertise are more likely to understand your business's unique challenges and opportunities and can often provide valuable advice and support.

Each type of lender has its strengths; for instance, big banks might offer more competitive rates, while community banks may provide more personalized service. As with any lender, you'll want to compare interest and terms. But the lender's reputation for customer service and other support services should also be taken into consideration. A responsive lender who communicates clearly and promptly can make obtaining and managing an SBA loan much smoother. Some lenders offer workshops, training, and advisory services to help you manage and grow your business. These services can be a valuable bonus when choosing a lender.

Stage Three: Submit Your Loan Package

You'll want to submit a comprehensive loan package to your chosen lender. This package typically includes your business plan, formal loan application, personal and business financial statements, tax returns, and collateral descriptions. Submitting a comprehensive loan package to your chosen lender is critical in the SBA loan application process. This package serves as the primary basis on which lenders assess your business's creditworthiness and determine your eligibility for a loan. To ensure that your loan package effectively represents your business and maximizes your chances of success, it should be meticulously prepared and organized.

When completing the loan application, clearly specify the amount you want to borrow and provide a detailed explanation of how the funds will be used. Be specific about the loan's needs, such as purchasing equipment, expanding operations, or refinancing existing debts. Typically, you'll also need to provide personal information for each principal owner of the business. This typically involves background information, such as addresses, names, social security numbers, and previous business experiences.

If you plan to use collateral to secure the loan, provide detailed descriptions of the assets you are willing to offer and include recent appraisals or valuation reports to substantiate the value of the assets listed as collateral. This can help speed up the loan review process and bolster your credibility.

Depending on your business structure and nature, you may also need to provide relevant legal documents such as articles of incorporation, leases, franchise agreements, and business licenses. Most lenders will require a detailed schedule of existing business debts, including creditor names, outstanding amounts, monthly payment details, and maturity dates.

Stage Four: SBA Review

Once your lender has reviewed and approved your loan application, the next crucial step involves the Small Business Administration (SBA) itself. The process through which the SBA reviews and ultimately approves your loan is integral to securing SBA-backed financing. Understanding this step can help you anticipate what to expect and ensure your application is as robust as possible.

In addition to the loan material you provided to your lender, they will include a specific application for the SBA guaranty. This application outlines the loan amount, the purpose, and the details about your business and its owners.

One of the first steps the SBA takes is verifying your loan eligibility. This includes checking compliance with SBA loan program criteria such as business size, type of business, use of loan proceeds, and owner's equity investment.

Next, the SBA reviews the submitted documents in detail to assess the viability of the business and the risk associated with the loan. This review includes a thorough examination of the financial health of your business as demonstrated by your financial statements and projections. They scrutinize the business plan to understand the business model, market opportunity, competitive landscape, and management team capabilities.

If collateral is part of the loan agreement, the SBA will review the descriptions and valuations provided to ensure they are adequate to secure the loan in case of default. This step is crucial in mitigating the SBA's risk and ensuring the loan is sufficiently backed.

Then, the SBA performs its credit and risk analysis, even though the lender may have already done so. This includes reviewing the credit histories of the business and its principal owners. The SBA's analysis helps ensure that all possible financial risks have been considered and that the business can reasonably repay the loan.

Finally, if the SBA is satisfied with their review and analysis, they will approve the loan's guarantee. This guarantee means that the SBA agrees to repay a portion of the loan to the lender should the borrower default. Both the borrower and the lender will be notified of the SBA's decision, and the lender will finalize the loan terms and proceed to disburse the funds according to the agreed-upon terms.

Get Professional Advice

Seeking professional advice when preparing an SBA loan application can be crucial in enhancing your chances of success. A financial advisor familiar with a business's needs, especially if they understand SBA loans, can provide invaluable insights into your financial health and readiness to take on debt.

Look for credentials such as a certified public accountant (CPA) or a certified financial planner (CFP), which indicate a high level of expertise. Accounting professionals can help you understand your financial statements in depth and identify areas for improvement before applying for a loan.

The more information you provide to an advisor, the better they can assist you, so be sure to gather all your financial statements and information before you visit. The right advisor can help you create robust financial projections that are realistic and align with your business goals. They can also help you gather and organize the necessary documentation, ensuring

> **The more information you provide to an advisor, the better they can assist you.**

that all financial data is accurate, complete, and presented in a manner that meets the SBA's requirements.

The SBA has designated certain lenders as Preferred Lenders Program (PLP). SBA-approved lenders possess specific knowledge of the requirements and intricacies of the SBA loan programs, giving them the expertise and experience necessary to navigate the complexities of loan applications, ensuring you meet all requirements and maximize the strength of your application. They can also provide targeted advice based on your business sector and financial needs. These institutions know what the SBA looks for and have the authority to process, close, service, and liquidate most SBA-guaranteed loans without prior SBA review. Working with a PLP can expedite the loan approval process.

Real-World Examples and Case Studies

We've seen many entrepreneurs use SBA-guaranteed loans to jumpstart their success. One tech startup used an SBA 7(a) loan to cover initial operating costs, including leasing office space and purchasing equipment. Another small manufacturing company obtained a 504 loan to purchase additional machinery and expand its production capacity, significantly increasing its market share. A family-owned restaurant used an SBA disaster loan to rebuild and reopen after a natural disaster, helping to retain jobs and stabilize the local economy.

Key Takeaways

- The United States Small Business Administration guarantees loans for qualifying businesses based on a number of employees or annual revenue.

- Consult a financial professional or use the resources provided by the SBA and their preferred lenders to prepare your application and decide which program is right for your business needs.

- Create a strong business plan, as described in Chapter Seven. It should outline your business analysis, market analysis, management background, and financial projections. This might be one of the critical elements of any form of business financing.

- Improve and maintain your creditworthiness. Your personal and business credit scores are key factors in the approval process. If you need assistance raising your score, reread our tips in the previous chapter.

9

When to Transition from Employee to Entrepreneur

Transitioning from working for someone else to working for yourself can be a life-changing decision. Entrepreneurs aren't just shifting careers; the move requires a transformation in mindset and lifestyle.

From financial preparation and skill enhancement to legal considerations and strategic planning, each step will strengthen your foundation for your new path. By following these carefully outlined strategies, you'll confidently navigate the transition, knowing you're well-prepared to meet the challenges and seize the opportunities in your entrepreneurial journey.

Financial Preparation

Before making the leap, be certain you have enough savings to cover your living expenses for several months, if not longer. Building a financial cushion is one of the most critical steps in transitioning from employment to entrepreneurship. It acts as a safety net cushion for the financial impact during the early stages of business development when cash flow might be unpredictable and initial expenses can be higher than expected.

> **Building a financial cushion is one of the most critical steps in transitioning from employment to entrepreneurship.**

A financial cushion will

- **Reduce financial stress and anxiety,** allowing you to focus on growing your business rather than worrying about immediate financial survival.

- **Provide operational flexibility**, giving you the breathing room to navigate unforeseen costs and delays without the pressure of immediate profitability.

- **Enhance your creditworthiness,** demonstrating to creditors that you possess prudence and preparedness, which are crucial traits for a successful entrepreneur.

The process begins with assessing your needs. How much money will you need to cover personal living expenses and business operations for a specific period? Most experts recommend saving for at least six months to one year of expenses. Next, set clear, achievable savings goals with monthly or weekly targets to make the process manageable and consistent.

You'll also want to review and adjust your personal and potential business budgets. Identify areas where you can cut back to accelerate your savings rate. This might include reducing discretionary spending, renegotiating bills, or finding cheaper alternatives for essential services. To speed up the process, look for ways to increase your income while still employed. This could involve freelance work, finding a higher-paying job, or working overtime. The additional income can be directed straight into your savings.

Strategically setting up automatic transfers from your checking account to a savings account can help you remain consistent with your contributions and prevent the temptation to spend the money elsewhere. While you want your savings to be accessible in an emergency, keeping them in a separate account from your everyday funds can reduce the temptation to dip into them for non-essential expenses. Consider using a high-yield savings account that offers better returns than a regular one but allows access when needed.

Importance of Reducing Personal Debt

Another crucial strategy for improving financial stability and increasing attractiveness to potential lenders or investors is reducing personal debt. Lowering your debt levels frees up more of your income for essential expenses and investments in your business. This increased financial flexibility allows you to adapt more easily to the unpredictable cash flows that characterize many new ventures.

Reducing your debt, particularly your credit utilization ratio (the amount of credit you use relative to your credit limits), can also significantly improve your credit score. A higher credit score increases your likelihood of securing business financing under favorable terms. Additionally, lower debt levels decrease your overall financial risk. Lenders and investors typically prefer to invest in or lend to entrepreneurs with a solid financial footing.

To reduce your personal debt, begin by taking an inventory of all your debts, including credit cards, student loans, auto loans, and mortgages. Track the interest rates, monthly payments, and remaining balances for each. This will allow you to prioritize your debts.

Two Main Methods of Effective Repayment

- **The Avalanche Method** focuses on paying off debts with the highest interest rates first while maintaining minimum payments on others. This method saves you money on interest over time.

- **The Snowball Method** pays off smaller debts first, so you can gain momentum as each balance is cleared, which can provide motivational wins.

You can also allocate extra money from your budget toward debt repayment. Even small additional amounts can significantly shorten your payoff period and reduce the total interest paid. Refinancing high-interest loans can also help you reduce your debt sooner. The lower interest rate can be particularly effective for credit card debts, where balance transfer options to lower or zero-interest cards are available.

If you have multiple sources of high-interest debt, debt consolidation can be a practical option. This involves taking out a new loan at a lower interest rate to pay off several higher-rate debts, simplifying your payments, and reducing interest costs. Finally, reassess your budget to find areas to cut expenses and redirect funds toward debt repayment. Even temporary cuts in discretionary spending can accelerate your debt reduction efforts.

Reducing debt eases the transition from employee to employer and positions you for more sustainable business growth, allowing you to focus on your entrepreneurial goals rather than financial burdens.

Skill and Knowledge Development

As you prepare to transition from W2 to independence, do whatever you can to make sure you have the specific skills required for the kind of business you want to pursue. You might need more technical abilities or managerial expertise. While you may already possess some of the skills necessary to embark on the business that interests you the most, you can always enhance your relevant skills. The skill sets can vary significantly depending on your chosen industry and the nature of your business. Developing skills and gaining knowledge in your respective field bolsters your ability to manage your business effectively and increases your credibility with potential investors, partners, and customers.

Start by analyzing the specific requirements of the business you plan to start. If it's a tech startup, software development or digital marketing skills might be crucial. For a retail business, supply chain management and customer service expertise could be more relevant. List the skills crucial for your business's success.

Next, conduct a personal skills audit to compare your current skills with those required for your business. Identify any gaps that hinder your ability to launch and manage your business effectively.

To bridge the gap, consider enrolling in relevant courses or programs. Many community colleges, universities, and online platforms offer targeted courses in areas like business administration, marketing, finance, and technology. MBA programs or specialized entrepreneurial courses can also provide comprehensive business training.

Certain professional certifications may enhance your knowledge and credibility, depending on your industry. For instance, a Project Management Professional (PMP) certification could be invaluable for someone starting a project management firm, while a Certified Public Accountant (CPA) credential benefits those starting a financial services business.

Your professional network can help you find continuous learning opportunities. Workshops, seminars, and other training events often provide more focused and less time-consuming training than formal courses and can provide up-to-date information on industry trends and technologies. Online learning platforms like Coursera, Udemy, or LinkedIn Learning offer a wide range of courses at various skill levels. Many of these courses are created and taught by industry experts and provide practical, skill-based learning.

Hands-on training is one of the best forms of education as you prepare for your transfer. Find a place to receive direct experience in the industry where you plan to start your business. This can involve working in a similar business, taking on relevant projects in your current job, or even volunteer work.

Mentors with experience in your industry can provide practical advice, insights, and guidance on essential skills and how to acquire them. Additionally, you could start small projects or a mini-version of your business idea as a side hustle. This business trial can be invaluable, helping you apply your skills in real-world scenarios and identify any additional training needs. Peers in your network can also share their mistakes and successes to enhance your learning curve.

Even after you make the transition, you'll want to stay updated on the new skills and information available in your industry. Industries evolve; new technologies, trends, and regulatory changes can quickly render yesterday's knowledge obsolete. Continuous learning helps you stay relevant and competitive, and because you're already in business, you can immediately apply the techniques you learn and adjust them to your specific situation.

You'll also want to develop your skills in leadership and management. Share these valuable insights with your team. You can use formal presentations or informal discussions. This not only reinforces your learning but also enhances your team's capabilities. Creating a culture of continuous learning within your organization will encourage others to engage in their learning activities and share their insights with the rest of the team. Consider allocating a budget for team members to attend training relevant to their roles.

Don't forget to share your learning experiences with others in your network. This could include industry reports, new technologies, or business strategies. You might also work on collaborative projects to deepen professional relationships and create innovative solutions and business growth.

Research Your Industry

Don't underestimate the value of a deep understanding of the industry you are entering. Comprehensive market research can provide insights into potential challenges and opportunities, helping you make informed decisions.

This step enables aspiring entrepreneurs to identify current trends, challenges, and opportunities. Effective industry research can significantly reduce the risks associated with starting a new business.

Use your research to assess the size of the industry and its growth trajectory. Understanding whether you are entering a growing, stable, or declining market can influence many aspects of your business strategy, from marketing to expansion planning. You'll also want to identify and analyze your potential competitors. Look at those offering similar products or services and alternative solutions to the same customer needs. Evaluate their strengths and weaknesses, market share, and business models. This research will help you find your competitive edge and potential market gaps you can exploit.

Use your market research to stay informed about technological advancements that could impact or disrupt your industry.

You'll also be able to identify your potential customers, their needs, and how existing businesses are currently meeting these needs. Segmenting the customer base by demographics, psychographics, behavior, or other relevant factors can help tailor your marketing and sales strategies effectively.

Use your market research to stay informed about technological advancements that could impact or disrupt your industry. Being at the forefront of adopting new technologies can provide a significant competitive advantage. You will also be able to look at broader economic factors that may influence your industry, such as economic cycles, international trade conditions, and interest rates. These factors can affect consumer spending patterns and business investment. There are various ways to collect data. Surveys, interviews, or experiments provide primary information. You can also uncover amazing insights by contacting potential customers to understand their needs and preferences or interviewing industry experts and business owners.

Existing information from industry reports, market studies, academic papers, and news articles becomes a secondary place to conduct your research. Reputable sources such as industry associations, trade journals, and government databases can also provide valuable data.

You've probably noticed by now that networking falls into every segment of moving from employee to entrepreneur. Attending industry conferences, seminars, and networking events can provide firsthand insights and trends, as well as opportunities to ask questions directly to those already working in the industry. You can also network online through forums and social media. Engage in industry-specific online communities to access resources and stay up-to-date on industry trends and customer opinions.

After you've conducted your research, use the insights to make informed decisions about product development, pricing strategies, marketing campaigns, and more. You can identify potential risks, develop strategies to mitigate them, and use them to leverage gaps and opportunities to innovate and differentiate your business from competitors.

Comprehensive market research equips you with the knowledge to navigate potential challenges and seize opportunities, enabling you to make strategic decisions that align with market realities.

Balancing Your Day Job with Entrepreneurial Aspirations

Balancing your day job with entrepreneurial aspirations is a common challenge for many nascent entrepreneurs. Effective time management is crucial to ensure that both your employment and business ventures receive the attention they need without compromising one for the other. Utilize planning tools and techniques to maximize productivity.

Effective time management is crucial.

You might begin with time-blocking techniques, such as allocating specific time slots. Divide your day into dedicated blocks reserved for specific activities. You might set aside early mornings for deep work on your business, such as strategic planning or product development, while evenings might be reserved for operational tasks like responding to emails or updating your website. Many people do well when establishing a consistent routine to reinforce habits supporting productivity. If you dedicate the same time each day to a particular task, your mind adapts, potentially increasing efficiency during those periods. A digital calendar can help you map out your time blocks visually. Tools like Google Calendar or Microsoft Outlook can be particularly useful. Color-code different activities to get a clear picture of how your day, week, and month look. This visual approach can help ensure a balanced allocation of time between your job and business tasks.

You might also consider using the Eisenhower Matrix. This four-quadrant box helps you decide on and prioritize tasks by urgency and importance, sorting out less urgent and important tasks that you should either delegate or not do at all. At the start of each week, determine what key goals must be achieved both in your job and business and then break these down into daily tasks. Ensure that each day includes at least one task that moves your business forward. You'll also want to identify which tasks impact your business's growth most and allocate your best time slots to these activities. For example, if reaching out to potential clients is critical, schedule this during your peak energy times.

As you work toward transitioning, you'll need to maximize your productivity. This can best be accomplished by minimizing multitasking. Multitasking can reduce efficiency and increase mistakes. Concentrating on a single task can improve your work quality and help you complete tasks faster. You can also leverage task management tools like Asana, Trello, and Monday.com to help handle short-term and long-term jobs. They allow you to track progress, set deadlines, and even collaborate with others if your business involves a team. You can also automate repetitive tasks like social media posts, invoice generation, and tracking.

Concentrating on a single task can improve your work quality and help you complete tasks faster.

Your ideal schedule might take some time to perfect. Be willing to adjust your time blocks as you discover what works best for you and as your business needs evolve. Regularly review how well your schedule is working. Are you consistently meeting your goals for your job and business? Use these insights to tweak your schedule for better results.

By carefully planning how you allocate your time and focusing on what truly needs to be done, you can make meaningful progress in your business while excelling in your day job.

Set Achievable Goals

Breaking down your business development activities into small, manageable tasks that can be accomplished alongside your job duties will help you maintain momentum without overwhelming your schedule. Setting achievable goals is essential when balancing the demands of a day job with entrepreneurial aspirations.

Start with clearly defined, achievable goals. They will keep you focused on what needs to be done next and prevent the feeling of overwhelm that comes with the enormity of starting and running a business while managing a full-time job. Manageable goals also enhance your productivity. This strategy makes them less intimidating and more inviting to tackle. Plus, completing smaller tasks provides a sense of accomplishment and motivates you to continue progressing. On top of all this, smaller, well-defined tasks are easier to adjust or shift in your schedule if unexpected job duties or business opportunities arise.

To accomplish your goals most effectively, identify your larger business objectives and break them into smaller, actionable tasks. For example, if your goal is to launch a new product, break it down into research, product development, market testing, etc. Clear milestones for each project phase will also help you realize your goal. Milestones act as checkpoints that help you assess progress and recalibrate your approach if necessary.

Another strategy for reaching your milestones is to prioritize tasks. Project management techniques like The Critical Path Method can help you prioritize tasks based on their impact on your overall timeline. This helps you identify which tasks must be completed to move on to the next step. You also will need to prioritize based on the goal's urgency and importance. Focus on tasks crucial for your business's success and schedule them during your most productive hours.

The SMART Criteria provides a great strategy for setting goals. It encourages us to set aside goals that don't meet the rules for a SMART goal.

- **Specific:** Goals should be clear and specific, with a well-defined scope so you know exactly what you need to do.

- **Measurable:** Attach specific metrics or indicators to each goal to track your progress and know when you've achieved it.

- **Achievable:** Ensure that goals are realistic and attainable within your current resources and time constraints.

- **Relevant:** Each goal should contribute directly to your broader business objectives, ensuring every task has a purpose.

- **Time-bound:** Assign a deadline to each task to prevent procrastination and maintain momentum.

Finally, most goals succeed when regularly reviewed—either daily or weekly. Whichever time frame you choose, start the period with a quick review and identify which tasks need to be completed first. Doing this daily helps keep your goals at the forefront of your mind.

Accountability partners who expect a regular update and can motivate you to stay on track. A journal—written on paper or saved as a digital record—can also give you a sense of accomplishment and identify areas for improvement.

Create a Strategic Exit Plan

A phased approach might be the most popular transition plan for entrepreneurs. This plan allows them to gradually reduce their employment hours as their business gains traction, providing continued financial security as they build the business.

This strategic method assures the entrepreneur a steady income to cover personal and business expenses during the transition period. It reduces the financial pressure often associated with the early stages of a startup. At the same time, the phased approach lets the new business owner test the viability of their business idea in the market without the immediate risk of full financial commitment. Plus, it allows learning and adapting as the business grows. Entrepreneurs can apply insights and skills gained from their current jobs, redevelop their business plans as needed, and gradually implement the changes into their business practices.

To make this phase approach work, establish clear, concrete milestones that will trigger changes in your employment status. For example, you might reduce your work hours only after your business reaches a certain income level or after securing a predetermined number of clients. You'll also want a realistic timeline for the transition. Consider factors such as expected business growth, financial targets, and personal commitments. A detailed timeline helps you monitor progress and make adjustments as needed.

After you have your milestones in place, it's time to negotiate flexible working arrangements with your employer. If feasible, openly discuss your entrepreneurial plans with your employer. Many employers value transparency and even support their transitioning employees' aspirations by offering part-time or remote work opportunities.

When you begin to talk to your employer about moving into a more flexible role, focus on how flexible working arrangements can benefit the employer as well. Emphasize potential increases in productivity, lowered office costs for remote work, and your continued commitment to your job responsibilities. Support your request with data or examples where flexible working arrangements have led to increased productivity or job satisfaction. If applicable, present instances of your previous performance demonstrating your ability to manage work effectively outside traditional settings.

Use the timeline you created to give your employer a detailed work schedule that outlines when and how you will complete your work tasks. Include availability hours, check-in times, or how remote work would look on a daily basis. Your employer might also feel reassured if you suggest a flexible schedule for a trial period. This allows you and your employer to evaluate how well the arrangement works

Set up a dedicated workspace that is conducive to productivity.

and make adjustments before committing to the long term. Finally, outline how you will communicate and collaborate with your team and supervisors while working flexibly. Propose regular update meetings or the use of collaborative tools to ensure transparency.

Set up a dedicated workspace that is conducive to productivity. Ensure you have all the necessary tools and technology to perform your job efficiently. You'll also want to maintain regular routines as if you were in the office. Start your day at a set time, dress appropriately if video calls are part of your routine, and set boundaries with household members to minimize distractions.

Regularly assess the effectiveness of your flexible working arrangement. Look at your productivity levels, work quality, and overall work-life balance. Communicate openly with your employer about your progress and any challenges, and be willing to make adjustments based on feedback from your employer.

Other Transitional Considerations

Networking is an important part of each step in the entrepreneurial journey. Remember to actively engage when you join groups or attend events. Ask questions, offer insights, and follow up with individuals to establish deeper connections. Networking is a two-way street. Always consider how you can add value to others' businesses or professional lives—share your knowledge, provide referrals, or support their business activities.

Collaboration can be a tremendous way to enhance your transitional networking. Look for opportunities to work on projects with your network contacts. Collaborations can build your skills, extend your reach, and lead to new business opportunities.

Transitioning from employee to entrepreneur is both an exhilarating and stressful journey. The stress from uncertainties and demands associated with launching and growing a new business can impair both personal well-being and business success. Developing and maintaining effective stress management techniques will help you maintain your health and ensure your entrepreneurial efforts are productive.

Start by identifying the most stressful aspects of the transition. Financial uncertainty, workload management, and balancing multiple responsibilities can be triggers, but acknowledging their impact and recognizing how stress can affect your mental and physical health is the first step. Symptoms might include sleep disturbances, irritability, fatigue, or difficulty concentrating. Acknowledging these effects is the first step in managing them.

Regular physical activity is one of the most effective ways to reduce stress. Exercise releases endorphins, natural brain chemicals that enhance your sense of well-being. Even simple activities like walking or yoga for twenty to thirty minutes a day can have significant stress-relieving effects. Choose activities you enjoy to ensure they become a sustainable part of your life.

Regular physical activity is one of the most effective ways to reduce stress.

Resist the temptation to forego sleep to increase productivity. Sleep is crucial for restoring your body and mind, and lack of sleep can exacerbate stress and actually lower productivity. Seven to nine hours per night is recommended for most adults. Your sleep hygiene can be improved by establishing a regular bedtime routine, creating a comfortable sleep environment, staying hydrated, and minimizing screen time before bed.

Don't minimize the importance of leisure activities during your transitional phase. Whether reading, gardening, or spending time with family and friends, hobbies, mindfulness meditation, breathing exercises, and other relaxation techniques can provide a necessary break and reduce stress.

If stress becomes overwhelming, consider seeking professional help. Therapists or counselors can provide valuable strategies for coping with stress effectively. Entrepreneur support groups, where you can share your experiences and learn from others facing similar challenges, can also be effective. Sharing your concerns with peers can provide comfort and insights.

Taking care of yourself is not a luxury—it's critical to ensuring your long-term success and well-being in your entrepreneurial journey.

Key Takeaways

- Prepare a financial cushion to ease your transition from employee to entrepreneur.

- Reduce your personal debt and use strategic methods to increase your credit score.

- Increase your skills and knowledge as you move into the transition phase.

- Set achievable goals, including a strategic exit plan from your place of employment.

- Consider a phasing-out strategy as you transition from employee to entrepreneur.

10

Building Your Team

We've discussed networking many times on these pages, and we can't stress enough the part these fellow entrepreneurs play in helping you reach your goals. In addition to these colleagues, you'll need a team of professionals to walk with you on this journey.

The success of a new venture hinges on both the entrepreneur's individual capabilities and the strength and expertise of the team around them. The complexity of managing a business often demands specialized knowledge across various domains. Accountants, attorneys, and mentors bring essential expertise and guidance that can safeguard your business from legal pitfalls and financial mismanagement.

You Need an Accountant

Accountants are essential for managing your business's financial health. They help ensure the accuracy of your financial records. Poor accounting records lead to poor decisions. Accountants can also manage critical financial tasks such as bookkeeping, payroll, taxes, and financial reporting.

Beyond basic financial management, accountants can help ensure that your business adheres to all applicable tax laws and takes advantage of available tax deductions and credits. This compliance prevents costly penalties and fines associated with tax errors while optimizing your financial strategy to retain more earnings legally. This oversight also helps detect and prevent errors, fraud, or embezzlement, which can pose significant risks to your business.

Accountants also play a strategic role in business planning. They can assist in budget preparation, financial forecasting, and financial risk assessment. This support is vital for crafting a business plan that is realistic, achievable, and capable of attracting investors or lenders.

Should your business be selected for an audit by tax authorities or other regulatory bodies, accountants prepare the necessary documentation and can represent your interests. Their expertise in handling audits will reduce the risk of negative outcomes.

Most Entrepreneurs Need an Attorney

Attorneys are crucial for navigating the legal complexities that come with running a business. They can help form the business entity, draft and review contracts, secure intellectual property rights, and advise on compliance with labor laws and other regulatory requirements.

A skilled attorney can also foresee potential legal issues and help you take proactive steps to mitigate them. This might involve structuring agreements to protect your interests, advising on compliance to avoid governmental fines, or handling employment law matters to prevent costly litigation. They can help you understand the licenses, permits, and operational standards requirements and ensure these are met to avoid legal penalties.

A significant part of managing business risk involves contracts with vendors, employees, customers, and partners. Lawyers draft, review, and negotiate contracts to protect your interests, minimize liabilities, and clarify obligations. This prevents misunderstandings and disputes that could lead to legal actions.

A significant part of managing business risk involves contracts with vendors, employees, customers, and partners.

For businesses with intellectual property as a key asset, lawyers play an essential role in securing and protecting it. This includes filing for patents, trademarks, or copyrights and defending against infringement claims, which safeguards the business's assets and market position.

Lawyers also advise on employment laws to ensure that your hiring practices, workplace policies, and employee terminations do not violate any laws. Proper legal advice in this area can prevent expensive lawsuits related to discrimination, wrongful termination, or other workplace issues.

Should legal issues arise, an experienced attorney is invaluable in managing crises. Whether it's a dispute with a vendor, a lawsuit from a customer, or a regulatory investigation, having a competent attorney can mean the difference between a swift resolution and a prolonged, costly battle.

Mentors Are Invaluable

Mentors bring a wealth of experience and knowledge to guide you through the intricacies of starting and running a business. Experienced mentors can provide strategic insights and advice based on years of industry experience, helping you avoid common pitfalls and accelerate your path to success. Additionally, these experienced men and women often have extensive professional networks and can open doors that might otherwise be closed. They can introduce you to potential partners, customers, and even investors. Most importantly, because the entrepreneurial journey can be isolating and stressful, a mentor can also offer emotional support, helping you navigate the ups and downs of business ownership.

The role of experienced mentors in guiding new entrepreneurs cannot be overstated. Mentors have typically encountered and overcome numerous challenges during their own career journeys. They can forewarn you about common pitfalls and mistakes in the industry, helping you avoid costly errors that could set your business back. Unlike general business advice you might find in books or online, mentors can provide tailored advice relevant to your specific situation and challenges. This personalized guidance is often more actionable and impactful. With a mentor, you can learn in a short time what might otherwise take years to understand through trial and error. This accelerated learning curve can be crucial in gaining a competitive edge and achieving business goals faster.

Mentors can also help you refine your business model to ensure it is viable and competitive within your market. Based on their understanding of market dynamics and operational efficiencies, they can point out weaknesses or areas for improvement and provide valuable insights into market trends and industry shifts. This knowledge can help you better position your product or service, adapt to changing market conditions, and seize emerging opportunities.

When you begin working with a mentor, be clear about what you hope to gain from the relationship. Setting specific objectives and expectations from the outset can help ensure that you and your mentor are aligned and can work effectively together. Being proactive in seeking advice, asking questions, and discussing your challenges and successes can make the relationship especially valuable, and regular meetings or check-ins can help maintain its momentum.

Be open to receiving constructive feedback. Part of a mentor's role is to challenge your ideas and strategies to help you grow and improve. What can you offer back to your mentor? This might include insights into newer industry trends, technologies, or opportunities that could benefit their professional interests.

Building Your Network

Identifying the specific expertise your business requires is a critical first step in building an effective support network and ensuring that you have the right resources to address various challenges and opportunities. Ensure that your business goals are clearly communicated and understood by your professional advisors. This alignment helps them provide targeted advice and services that directly contribute to achieving these goals. Whether in the initial stages of setting up your business or looking to grow and expand, understanding and addressing these needs can significantly impact your operations and strategic decisions.

Conduct a thorough analysis of your business to understand its core operations, products or services, customer base, and industry. This assessment should be in your business plan and will highlight areas where specialized knowledge is crucial and where you might have gaps in your current capabilities. Distinguish between immediate and short-term needs—things necessary for daily operations—and long-term needs—elements essential for growth and scalability.

Consider how your needs might change as your business grows.

For example, legal compliance and accounting might be immediate needs, while strategic marketing and long-term financial planning may be crucial for future growth.

Consider how your needs might change as your business grows. For instance, what works for a solo entrepreneur or a small team may not suffice as you begin to grow. Eventually, you'll need a more sophisticated legal, HR, or financial strategy.

Depending on your industry, you may need advisors who understand specific technical aspects or market dynamics unique to your field. For instance, a tech startup might need IT security expertise, while a manufacturing business may benefit from supply chain management advice.

Speak with other entrepreneurs or business owners in your industry to gain insight into common challenges and the types of expertise needed to overcome them. This is another place where networking events and industry forums become invaluable.

Next, set up introductory meetings with the professionals you think your business will need. Accountants, lawyers, or business consultants can help identify areas where you can best use their services. Many professionals offer initial consultations free of charge or at a reduced rate. Additionally, these meetings can help you gauge their interest in helping your business so that when you begin the selection stage, you already have a few candidates.

Customer feedback can also highlight areas where your company needs improvement. They can identify holes in your customer service processes and product quality issues, giving you insight into the kinds of specific expertise to address. Regular reviews of your business performance, through metrics like sales, customer retention rates, and financial health, can signal spots where bolstering your capabilities with external expertise could be beneficial.

After you've identified your needs, choose professionals who have proven expertise and understand the entrepreneurial journey. Look for individuals who come highly recommended by other business owners and demonstrate a clear interest in your business's success.

Selecting the right professionals to support and guide your business is crucial. Before choosing these specialists, carefully check their credentials and qualifications. Make sure the companies and individuals you consider have certifications, licenses, and the formal education needed for their particular field. For example, accountants should ideally be CPAs (Certified Public Accountants), and lawyers should be members of the bar association in your jurisdiction.

Selecting the right professionals to support and guide your business is crucial.

Look for professionals with extensive experience, especially in your industry or in dealing with businesses at a similar stage of development. The professional you choose should also understand the challenges and nuances of entrepreneurship. In fact, those who possess the entrepreneurial spirit will be even more valuable. Experienced professionals are likely to be more adept at anticipating potential issues and navigating complex scenarios.

As you begin to narrow down your choices, look for professionals who communicate clearly and promptly and show a genuine interest in understanding and contributing to your business. Ensure that you feel comfortable discussing all aspects of your business with them. Listen for the candidates who ask insightful questions about your operations, goals, and challenges.

After you select your team of professionals, clearly communicate your expectations and objectives. Establishing clear guidelines and goals from the outset ensures both parties are aligned and can work effectively together. Then, maintain regular contact with your advisors. Frequent updates allow them to provide timely advice and help you stay ahead of potential issues. You might even create a calendar to schedule and track communications. This ensures you do not neglect anyone in your network and can plan your outreach efforts efficiently.

Engage these professionals early in the business planning process. Their insights in the first stages can be invaluable in setting up robust operational, financial, and legal frameworks. They can identify potential issues and risks—such as financial risks, legal compliance issues, or operational inefficiencies—and help you develop solutions or preventive measures before they become significant problems that could cost time and money to resolve.

Our network of professionals also may be able to provide insights regarding the competitive landscape and market positioning of your business based on their unique perspective, which is informed by their experience with other clients in similar or diverse industries. Legal professionals can help identify and protect intellectual property that could be crucial to your business's competitive advantage.

Be sure to involve your chosen professionals in your strategic planning sessions. Their input can ensure that all your plans are feasible from financial, operational, and legal perspectives. Establish clear communication channels and protocols from the start. Decide how and when updates, meetings, and reports will occur.

Other Potential Sources for Your Business Network

In addition to accountants, lawyers, and consultants, look for businesses that complement rather than compete with your own to engage with. This can include companies that offer products or services that align with or enhance your value proposition to customers. For instance, a software development company could partner with a hardware manufacturer to offer a more comprehensive tech solution.

Partnerships with these complementary businesses are particularly effective when both parties share a similar target audience. This alignment allows both businesses to cross-promote products or services to a broader audience without the cost of acquiring new customers. However, partnering with businesses with a reputation for quality and reliability is important. The reputation of your partners can reflect on your business, impacting your brand's perception.

As you build these partnerships, define clear objectives for what each party hopes to achieve. Whether expanding into new markets, enhancing product offerings, or leveraging each other's expertise, clear goals ensure the partnership is focused and measurable. It's also important to be certain the benefits of the partnership are mutual and significant for all involved parties. This could involve sharing resources like marketing databases, technology, or distribution channels, which can help reduce costs and increase reach. To keep everything clear, consider creating a formal agreement out-lining each party's roles, responsibilities, and contributions. This can prevent misunderstandings and conflicts. Legal documentation is particularly crucial in partnerships involving shared revenues or joint product development.

These kinds of partnerships allow you to collaborate on marketing initiatives such as joint advertising campaigns, bundled offerings, or co-hosted events. This gives you the leverage to multiply the marketing reach while sharing the costs. You can also use each other's sales channels to promote products or services. For instance, you can cross-promote by adding promotional material to each other's shipments, feature your partners' offerings on websites, or utilize each other's retail spaces.

You can also work together to enhance or develop new products or services that combine your expertise and capa-bilities. This kind of strategic partnership can create unique offerings that are more competitive and appealing to customers.

These professional networks also encourage referrals. This includes clients and mutual referrals among professionals like accountants, lawyers, and consultants who serve similar target markets. Building a robust referral network is a strategic approach to expanding your business reach and enhancing its reputation. By creating a system that encourages referrals, you can leverage the trust and credibility established with current clients and professional contacts to gain access to new cus-tomers more efficiently and cost-effectively. This network can include a diverse range of stakeholders, from clients to the various professionals you need to get your busi-ness off the ground. These kinds of partnerships can

> **Building a robust referral network is a strategic approach to expanding your business reach and enhancing its reputation.**

help you find those who understand the value your business provides and are ready to recommend your services to others in their network.

Referrals from your business partners come with built-in trust, significantly reducing the effort required to build credibility with new clients. A recommendation from a trusted source can often influence decisions more effectively than traditional marketing methods. They also represent cost-effective growth. Acquiring customers through referrals is generally less expensive than through other marketing channels. You can also expect higher conversion rates because they already have a positive impression of your business from the referrer.

In addition to complementary businesses, you can collaborate with clients who are delighted with your products or services. These individuals are more likely to recommend your business to others. Identify these referrers who have high levels of satisfaction and engage them actively.

To foster client referrals, consider setting up a formal referral program with incentives for those who bring new clients to your business. Rewards can be in the form of discounts, service upgrades, or even direct monetary incentives. And don't forget to thank your referrers. Recognizing their effort and contribution encourages continued support and fosters long-term relationships.

Using a good customer relationship management (CRM) system can provide great insights to track referrals, manage follow-ups, and analyze the effectiveness of your referral strategies. Plus, you can leverage professional networking platforms like LinkedIn to maintain connections, endorse skills, and publish content that your professional and client networks can easily share with potential referrals.

Finally, feedback loops within your network can provide essential information to help grow your business. You might have formal advisory meetings or informal catch-ups within your professional network or team. Use these opportunities to gather constructive feedback on business strategies, operational management, and customer engagement. Effective feedback loops also provide essential insights into how well your business strategies, operational management, and customer engagement tactics work, allowing for timely adjustments and informed decision-making. In addition to helping your business grow, engaging your team in feedback processes helps them feel valued and involved, which can enhance motivation and job satisfaction.

Feedback loops must be intentional.

Though feedback loops can be casual, they must be intentional. That's why scheduling regular meetings with your team to discuss various aspects of the business is vital. You could plan these weekly, bi-weekly, or monthly, depending on the needs of your business.

Many professionals neglect to collect feedback during one-on-one sessions. Often, these annual or semi-annual reviews are conducted to evaluate team members' performance; however, they are excellent opportunities to gather more personalized feedback about each person's work experiences, challenges, and suggestions for improvement. Don't dismiss survey tools like Google Forms or SurveyMonkey to conduct anonymous surveys among your team. Anonymity can help you collect honest and candid feedback, particularly on sensitive issues.

External feedback channels can also provide critical information on ways to improve your business. Implement systems for collecting customer feedback regularly through online reviews, customer surveys, or feedback forms. Make them easily accessible so customers can honestly share their experiences and opinions.

Some entrepreneurs set up an advisory board of mentors, industry experts, or business partners to provide strategic feedback on their business operations and plans. Others take advantage of industry networking events or peer review sessions to present aspects of their businesses and get feedback from fellow entrepreneurs and industry professionals.

It's imperative that you don't just let feedback sit in an inbox. Leveraging feedback includes systematically analyzing the data to identify common themes, patterns, and outliers. Data visualization software and other similar tools can help interpret the information more effectively.

Weigh all form data and verbal information carefully, considering the source and context. Not all feedback is equally useful or applicable. Be careful to discern which pieces should influence decision-making.

After you compile and evaluate the data, it's time to create an action plan to address the key areas of concern. Assign responsibilities and deadlines to ensure these plans are executed effectively. Be sure to inform your team and relevant stakeholders, including customers, about the changes you make in response to their feedback. This communication fosters a culture of transparency and collective ownership of business processes.

As with any modifications you make to your processes, you'll want to monitor the outcomes of the shifts you make. Assess the changes to be sure they are producing the desired effects. This means you'll get feedback on your feedback. Regularly invite comments and evaluations on how the feedback processes themselves can be improved. This meta-level feedback ensures that your mechanisms for gathering and acting on feedback evolve and remain effective.

Nurturing Relationships with Regular Communication

Regular communication with your professional network is essential for nurturing and maintaining strong relationships that can be beneficial to your business. This continuous engagement not only keeps your business at the forefront of your contacts' minds but also facilitates a flow of valuable information, advice, and opportunities.

Develop strategic partnerships that can offer mutual benefits. For example, a partnership with a marketing firm could enhance your visibility in the market while providing the firm access to your clientele.

Developing strategic partnerships is a powerful way to accelerate growth and expand the capabilities of your business. By collaborating with other businesses or professionals, you can leverage complementary strengths, resources, and customer bases, achieving heights you could never do alone.

It's easy for entrepreneurs to get busy trying to keep up with their own business; however, in those most hectic times, it's even more important to keep in regular contact with your network. Use online updates, emails, newsletters, or personal communications to keep your business at the top of their minds and provide value to those who refer you. This includes information, free tools or resources, and keep your eye out for reciprocal referrals.

Frequent interaction helps strengthen relationships and build trust and familiarity. Strong relationships are more likely to yield beneficial partnerships, referrals, and collaboration opportunities. These could lead to new projects, joint ventures, or expanded customer bases.

To maintain strong relationships, we must be willing to adapt the terms of our partnerships as they evolve. Each business's needs and capabilities may change over time, requiring adjustments to the partnership agreement. You can do this by regularly reviewing the partnership's performance against the set objectives. Use metrics such as sales growth, customer feedback, or market expansion to evaluate the partnership's success.

To maintain strong relationships, we must be willing to adapt the terms of our partnerships as they evolve.

Building a relationship based on mutual understanding and trust is crucial for long-term collaboration. Invest time developing these relationships, as they can become one of your most valuable business assets.

Every time you recognize and appreciate the contributions of others in your team or network, you build trust and caring. This can be through acknowledgment of business successes, referrals, or more formal appreciation events. Showing appreciation for your professional network is crucial for fostering lasting relationships and encouraging ongoing support, reciprocity, and collaboration. Recognition and gratitude reinforce the value you place on these relationships, which can lead to increased loyalty, more frequent referrals, and a stronger willingness to assist you in the future.

There's nothing like being known as someone who acknowledges and appreciates others to enhance your reputation within your industry. This spread of knowledge makes customers more eager to connect and other businesses more ready to collaborate.

One form of recognition that has gone by the wayside in our age of digital communication is a handwritten thank-you note. It shows thoughtfulness and effort, making it a powerful way to express gratitude. For more immediate or less formal recognition, a well-crafted thank-you email can also be effective. Be specific about what you are thanking the person for, which reinforces the value of their contribution.

Publicly showing gratitude on social media demonstrates your appreciation and highlights your connection to others in your network, potentially bringing them recognition and opportunities. Recognizing contributors in your newsletters, on your website, or during events such as webinars, seminars, or networking gatherings can provide significant public acknowledgment.

You could also send small gifts. Whether it's a gift card, a book related to their interests, or another thoughtful item, these meaningful trinkets are excellent ways to show gratitude. Be sure the gift is appropriate and proportional to the nature of the help or support you received. Inviting your contacts to special events, whether professional or casual, can also be a great way to express appreciation. It can also provide them networking opportunities, adding value to the gesture. Don't put your logo or name on the gift. Instead, personalize the gift to the recipient. Then, each time they see or use your gift, they will think about you and your relationship.

One of the most impactful ways to show appreciation to other businesses in your network is to support your contact's endeavors in return. This could involve referring clients to them, supporting their events, or providing expertise and resources when they need it. Endorsements or testimonials, especially on professional platforms like LinkedIn, can boost your network contacts' professional profiles while showing your appreciation for their contributions to your business.

These acts of appreciation should be timely and personalized. Prompt acknowledgment immediately reinforces positive behavior, and personalized gestures show that you pay attention to the person's interests and preferences, making the appreciation more impactful and sincere.

Reciprocal support is one of the best and most appreciated ways to show gratitude to your business network. It builds trust, strengthens loyalty, and often results in reverse reciprocity. When you support your partners' events and patronize their businesses, you also increase your visibility within the community. This can lead to new connections and opportunities. Plus, being seen as a supportive and collaborative professional enhances your reputation, making others more inclined to recommend your services or collaborate with you in the future.

> **Reciprocal support builds trust, strengthens loyalty, and often results in reverse reciprocity.**

To effectively refer clients, you need a good understanding of what your network members offer and their target markets. Sincere interest in your network will boost this potential. It's also a good practice to actively look and listen for opportunities to refer clients. This could be as straightforward as recommending a network member's services in relevant conversations or sharing their contact information with potential clients. And to enhance your reputation, follow up to see how it went after you make a referral. This feedback will be valuable for you and your network members and help refine future referrals.

You can also use platforms like LinkedIn to endorse the skills of your network members or provide recommendations. Be as specific as possible when making recommendations. This public endorsement not only boosts their professional profile but also shows your active support for their career.

It's vital as you provide reciprocal support to continually check yourself to ensure your support is genuinely intended to help others, not just to receive something in return. Authenticity in your actions fosters deeper and more meaningful connections. The key is to provide support consistently. Consistent support is more likely to be remembered and reciprocated than sporadic help.

Reciprocal support is a cornerstone of building and maintaining a strong professional network. By actively supporting the professional growth of your network members, you create a positive cycle of mutual benefit. This approach not only enhances the value of your network but also establishes you as a key contributor to a thriving professional community.

Key Takeaways

- **Building and leveraging a professional network is a dynamic and strategic process critical to your business's growth.**

- **Every business needs key professionals to help them succeed.** Unless you have the skills of an attorney or a CPA, you'll need to add these to your business network.

- **Mentors are essential to the success of your business.**

11

Sustaining Success and Planning for the Future

As your business moves beyond its initial stages and starts to stabilize, sustaining success and planning for future growth become crucial. Strategies for maintaining momentum and effectively planning for the future can help ensure that your business not only survives but thrives in the long term.

Maintaining Momentum in Your New Business Venture

A successful business is an evolving and growing organism. This means entrepreneurs must constantly look for ways to improve products, services, and operational processes and remain responsive to customer feedback and market trends.

They must also be willing to adapt and innovate as needed. Implementing a culture of continuous improvement ensures that your business remains competitive and responsive to changing market conditions.

The feedback loops you establish will become a key to your business's growth and adaptive moves. In addition to listening to customers, employees, mentors, and peers, you can also use Key Performance Indicators (KPIs) to systematically assess the efficiency and effectiveness of various aspects of your business.

Remember that a change in mindset is imperative for the entrepreneur and must trickle down through the organization. Successful continuous improvement is actively supported by top management and championed by leaders in the company.

Engage employees at all levels in the continuous improvement process by encouraging a mindset of agility where employees feel empowered to respond quickly to feedback and changes in the market. This will flatten hierarchies to some extent, speeding up decision-making processes and providing teams with the tools and authority they need to make adjustments. You can also promote a culture where mistakes are viewed as opportunities for learning rather than occasions for punishment. Encourage open discussions about failures and missteps as a way to glean insights and prevent future errors.

In that same vein, you can foster an environment where innovation is valued and rewarded. Give employees space to come up with innovative solutions to improve products, services, or processes. Consider setting aside time and resources for employees to work on project ideas that could benefit the business. This can be facilitated through workshops, seminars, webinars, courses, and professional development programs that align with the emerging needs of the business and teach employees how to identify improvement opportunities and implement solutions effectively.

Standardize the processes you create as the improvements are identified. This brings consistency and efficiency across your organization. Implement small groups or teams who regularly meet to identify, analyze, and solve work-related problems. This technique, borrowed from Japanese management practices, can enhance ownership and collaboration among team members.

A system of incentives to reward individuals and teams for their contributions to improvement efforts can boost this mindset of continuous improvement. Recognition can take many forms, from public acknowledgment and awards to bonuses and promotions. When we celebrate successes, big and small, we reinforce the value of continuous improvement within the organization.

Implementing a culture of continuous improvement is about creating an environment where ongoing enhancement is part of the daily operation. By integrating continuous assessment, responsive adaptation, and systematic processes into the fabric of your organization, you can ensure that your business not only adapts to current challenges but also proactively prepares for future demands, maintaining its competitiveness and relevance in the market.

Customer Retention Strategies

To truly scale, entrepreneurs need to develop and implement strategies aimed at retaining customers. Loyalty programs can prove to be an effective way to create customer satisfaction. These programs reward customers for repeat purchases or referrals. This can be in the form of points, discounts, or special offers. The most effective rewards are tailored to align with your customers' preferences and purchasing behaviors.

Many businesses use a tiered loyalty system where customers earn more significant rewards as they reach higher spending thresholds. This encourages continued engagement and increases customer lifetime value.

Customers develop loyalty and regularly pass out referrals because the business gives exceptional customer service. Customers appreciate quick response times when handling inquiries and resolving issues. They also enjoy personalized support. You can analyze data to understand buying patterns, preferences, and pain points. Then, use this data to tailor your marketing, sales, and support efforts to better meet the needs of your existing customers.

When team members recognize repeat customers, call them by name, understand their purchase history, and anticipate their needs, you enhance the customer experience.

Remain proactive with your customers. Don't wait for customers to reach out with problems. Instead, use data to identify potential issues and reach out proactively to solve them. This prevents dissatisfaction and demonstrates your commitment to customer care.

Customers enjoy free or discounted access to workshops, webinars, or events that provide educational content relevant to your products or services. This adds value and strengthens the customer's relationship with your brand. Plus, exclusive offers or content available only to existing customers makes customers feel valued and encourages repeat business.

Regular engagement through social media and email marketing can also help keep your brand in the minds of your customers. Be sure to interact with customers and respond to messages promptly.

Regular newsletters or emails provide value beyond just sales promotions. You can include useful content such as tips, industry news, or early access to new products. Be sure to personalize emails to address customers by name and tailor content based on their past purchases or preferences.

You can also use email marketing and social media campaigns to fuel your feedback loop. Showing you value customer opinions and are willing to make changes based on their feedback increases loyalty. When you update products or services based on customer feedback, share this information and let customers know their comments and suggestions directly influence improvements. Retaining an existing customer is more cost-effective than acquiring a new one.

Clearly defining and communicating your brand's identity, values, and unique selling proposition is attractive to customers. A strong, well-defined brand can differentiate your business from competitors and command a premium in the market. Create strategies that enhance brand visibility and reputation. This can include digital marketing, public relations, and community involvement. A well-known and respected brand is more attractive to potential buyers or investors.

A strong, well-defined brand can differentiate your business from competitors.

Don't forget to protect your brand through trademarks and copyrights. Secure intellectual property that contributes to your brand's unique offerings, as this can add substantial value to your business during a sale. Effective retention strategies not only ensure ongoing revenue but also build brand loyalty and advocacy among your customer base.

Customer retention strategies are crucial for sustaining business success. By focusing on loyalty programs, exceptional customer service, regular engagement, and continuously adding value through educational content, you can maintain a strong, loyal customer base. These strategies help retain customers and transform them into advocates for your brand, thereby driving organic growth through word-of-mouth and increased customer lifetime value.

Performance Monitoring

In your business plan, you identified goals and benchmarks and ways you plan to monitor performance. Follow this roadmap and add KPIs as they become relevant. Monitor performance to gauge your business's health and understand how well you are achieving your objectives.

Set up systems for regular data collection. This might involve automated tools, software that integrates with your sales platforms, or manual tracking methods, depending on the nature of the KPI.

Schedule regular meetings with your team to review KPIs. These could be weekly, monthly, or quarterly, depending on the operational dynamics of your business and the specific KPIs in question. Software dashboards and data visualization tools can make the KPI data easy to understand and analyze. Tools like Tableau, Microsoft Power BI, or even Excel dashboards can help present the data in an actionable format.

Look for upward or downward trends in the KPI data. These can help pinpoint areas where the business is performing well or where it may be facing challenges. Compare your performance against benchmarks and industry standards. This comparison can highlight where your business stands in relation to competitors and industry averages. After you identify performance issues, use root cause analysis to dig deeper into why certain areas are underperforming. This might involve looking at additional data, revisiting the strategies employed, or soliciting feedback from customers or staff.

Use the insights you gain from performance monitoring to make strategic adjustments. This could involve reallocating resources, changing processes, or introducing new strategies. A culture of continuous improvement will use insights from performance monitoring and feedback loops to make incremental improvements regularly.

Regularly reviewing business performance lets you make data-driven decisions and gain valuable insights into the health and efficiency of your operations. This proactive approach helps sustain business growth and efficiency. It can also produce long-term sustainability and success.

Invest in Your Team

As your business grows and operations expand, you'll need a bigger, more proficient team. Invest in training and development to enhance their skills and keep them motivated. Investing in your team helps ensure your business's long-term success and growth, and maintains operational efficiency while driving innovation.

Regular training ensures that your team's skills remain up-to-date with the latest industry standards and technologies and helps maintain your business's competitive edge. Employees who receive training and personal development opportunities tend to be more satisfied and loyal to the company, reducing turnover and the associated costs of hiring and training new staff. A well-trained and knowledgeable team is more likely to contribute innovative ideas and effective solutions to problems, driving the business forward.

Regularly assess the skill gaps within your team. Use performance reviews, direct feedback, and observations of day-to-day operations to identify and tailor the necessary training programs. Diverse learning opportunities such as on-the-job training, formal courses, workshops, and seminars will help cover your team's various learning styles and availability. Online learning platforms also offer flexibility and a wide range of subjects.

Regularly assess the skill gaps within your team.

Personal growth opportunities can be a tremendous investment in your leadership team. Work with your team members to create personalized career development plans. Align these plans with the individual's career goals and the company's needs, outlining a clear path for progression within the organization. Potential leaders within your team will benefit from leadership training and mentorship opportunities. This helps to prepare them for future management roles and succession planning.

Recognition and rewards programs provide motivation, especially when tied to performance and achieving specific training goals. Public recognition can enhance motivation and encourage a culture of excellence.

Where possible, include interactive and hands-on components in your training sessions. This could include simulations, role-playing, or real-world projects that allow employees to apply what they've learned in a practical setting. Peer-to-peer learning, where team members share knowledge and skills with each other, not only enhances learning but also builds team cohesion.

As with every aspect of your business, regularly evaluate the effectiveness of your training programs through feedback surveys, assessments, and by measuring performance improvements. Use this data to refine and improve future training.

A skilled and engaged workforce will help maintain your business's operational efficiency and innovation capacity. Investing in your team is not just about providing training; it's about fostering an environment that values continuous learning, professional growth, and recognition. By implementing effective training programs, supporting career development, and creating a culture that rewards learning and improvement, you can ensure that your team remains capable, motivated, and committed to the success of your business..

Is Scaling Your Business in Your Future?

Before deciding to scale, thoroughly assess whether your business model, supply chain, and team can handle increased demand. Consider the financial implications and the need for additional resources or technology.

The first step is analyzing the current viability and profitability of your business model. In the same way you explored feasibility before starting your business, you'll need to examine those same elements as you grow. Can your core product or service generate sustained revenue—even when scaled? Will your unit economics make sense on a larger scale? What changes might be needed to maintain profitability?

You'll continue to repeat the steps you followed when you embarked on your business. This means the next step is to research the market to validate continued demand at a larger scale. Look for trends that demonstrate whether the market is expanding or contracting and assess the potential market size to ensure it can support a larger operation. Customer surveys or other means of collecting data can be extremely useful. You'll also need to evaluate your existing supply chain capacity. Can your suppliers handle increased production or service volumes? You'll need to assess your suppliers' ability to meet larger orders and evaluate the robustness of your logistics and distribution networks.

Identify any potential risks associated with scaling your current supply chain. Are you dependent on a limited number of suppliers? Will you face logistical challenges in new markets? Can your supply chain adapt to changes, such as new product lines or shifts in customer demand?

Assess whether your current team has the capacity and skills to manage increased operational demands. Identify gaps and provide additional team members or training where necessary. Evaluate the ability of your leadership and management team to handle a larger organization. Expansion might mean strengthening leadership skills, refining management structures, or bringing in experienced executives.

Scaling requires calculating the additional funds you'll need to expand production, marketing, staffing, and infrastructure. As you plan for growth, project your cash flow to ensure you can manage expenses through the scaling phase without jeopardizing operational integrity. Consider scenarios where receivables might be delayed or where capital expenditures increase.

Growth also affects your systems. Can your current technological infrastructure support larger operations? Review your IT systems, manufacturing equipment, and customer service platforms. Your review might reveal a need to make an investment in your technological requirements. You might also need a larger ERP system, e-commerce platform, or better automation. Assess the ROI of these investments and their impact on your operational efficiency.

Consider engaging with consultants or advisors specializing in scaling businesses. They can provide an unbiased view of your readiness and suggest practical strategies to address any gaps. You may want to run pilot programs in limited markets or product lines to test the scalability of your operations. This can provide valuable insights and allow you to adjust before a full-scale rollout. Remember to implement feedback mechanisms during the scaling process so you can make relevant real-time adjustments.

Strategic expansion is a critical phase in a business's growth trajectory, requiring careful planning to ensure each step stays aligned with your overall business strategy and market conditions. Whether considering new markets, increasing production capacity, or extending your product lines, each step needs to be meticulously planned and executed to ensure sustainable growth.

Strategic expansion is a critical phase in a business's growth trajectory.

Analyze how the expansion aligns with your overall business strategy. If expansion leverages your company's strengths and aligns with your strategic goals, you'll need to decide which approach you want to take.

Earlier, we discussed the phase approach to scaling. Gradually increasing your presence allows you to test the waters before fully committing significant resources. Other entrepreneurs use the Big Bang Approach. In cases where market conditions are rapidly changing or highly competitive, a more aggressive expansion might be necessary. This means you'll need a significant initial investment and swift action to capture market share quickly.

Regardless of the approach you choose, you'll need to identify potential funding sources, much like in the building days of your business, and develop detailed budgets that account for additional costs such as marketing, staffing, technology upgrades, and possible operational inefficiencies during the transition period.

If you're planning to enter new geographic markets, you'll want to customize your product offerings, marketing strategies, and operations to fit local tastes, cultural nuances, and regulatory requirements. New markets also add opportunities to form strategic partnerships or alliances with local businesses that can provide market insights, distribution networks, and credibility.

Use Diversification to Drive Your Business's Expansion

Diversification is a strategic approach used to manage risk by spreading investment and operational focus across different products, services, or markets. This strategy can buffer a business against potential losses in any one area. By reducing your reliance on a single source of revenue, if one product line or market encounters difficulties, the business can still generate revenue from other areas. This can be especially important in industries subject to seasonal fluctuations or economic cycles. Additionally, exploring new markets, product areas, service models, or alternative customer segments that align with your business's strengths and market trends can uncover opportunities for growth that were not apparent within the original business focus.

Like every business strategy, entrepreneurs will have to take time to do market research before diversifying. Demographic studies, customer surveys, and competitive analysis will help you understand where opportunities for growth and profitability lie. At the same time, you want diversification that is compatible with your current business operations and core competencies. Be sure to build on existing strengths or involve manageable extensions of your business's capabilities.

Before you diversify, perform a detailed financial analysis to evaluate the costs associated with diversifying as well as the potential benefits. This includes startup costs, potential market share, revenue forecasts, and profitability timelines. You might need to allocate funds for innovation, research, and development. Use this analysis to ensure that pursuing new opportunities does not unduly strain your current business's resources or compromise its performance.

Every move in your business presents risks.

Every move in your business presents risks, so you'll need to clearly identify potential challenges and develop strategies to mitigate them. These strategies might include phased market entry, partnerships with established businesses in the new market, or incremental product development to test market receptiveness.

Before fully committing to a diversification strategy, consider conducting pilot projects or limited product releases. This allows you to gather real-world data on the strategy's viability. Feedback will always be a valuable tool for refining your approach before initiating a full rollout. This iterative process can significantly reduce financial risk and increase the chances of successful diversification.

Your diversification strategy should include ways to identify and exploit synergies between new and existing business lines. This could involve shared marketing efforts, combined distribution logistics, or cross-selling opportunities. Your team also needs to be adequately prepared and trained to handle these new operations or market engagements. You might need to hire new staff with specific expertise or provide additional training to existing employees.

Your new market may require you to set up specific KPIs to track your success relative to expectations. Entrepreneurs must be ready to pivot or adjust based on performance and changing market conditions.

Diversification may open doors for partnerships and collaborations. Engage with universities, research institutions, or other companies to co-develop new products or services and look for innovative ideas in other industries that could be adapted to your own. Every entrepreneur can benefit from fresh ideas and expertise that complement their capabilities. This cross-pollination of ideas can lead to unique product offerings or service models.

You can use diversification to establish an organizational culture that encourages creativity and experimentation among employees. This might involve setting up innovation labs, hosting hackathons, or providing time and resources for employees to work on passion projects. It can also help you develop a tolerance for calculated risks and acceptance that not all innovative efforts will succeed. A supportive approach to failure helps foster a more innovative mindset among your team. Sharing what they learn from both successful and failed innovation efforts can improve future projects and help build a resilient approach to innovation.

Don't forget to monitor the KPIs and scalability potential for your new product or service. This diversification could lead to additional expansion, but you'll need to evaluate if it can be done without compromising quality or significantly increasing costs.

It's Never Too Early to Consider Exit Strategies

It may seem premature to consider exit strategies while you're still on someone else's payroll. However, entrepreneurs who grow, scale, and diversify often find themselves in a position to sell. This planning allows you to exit in a way that maximizes the value of your business and secures your financial future. Even if the prospect of exiting seems distant or uncertain, a clear exit plan provides a roadmap for securing your financial future when the time comes.

Life is unpredictable. Market changes, health issues, or other personal reasons might necessitate an unexpected exit. Your exit plan prepares you for any situation. It also can influence key business decisions. For example, if you plan to sell to a larger corporation, you might focus on aligning your operations with industry standards that appeal to such buyers. On the other hand, if you plan to retire and make your business a family legacy, you'll pay close attention to which of your children or other heirs should be brought into the business early.

Creating an exit plan allows you to implement strategies that can gradually increase the value of your business over time, making it more attractive to potential buyers or investors when you decide to sell.

Begin by deciding what you want to achieve with your exit. This could be financial security, starting a new venture, or simply retiring. Understanding your personal goals will guide the type of exit strategy you pursue. You'll also want to consider what you hope to see happen to the business after your exit. Do you want it to continue to grow under new leadership, or are you comfortable seeing it merge with another company?

Options for Exiting

- **Sell to a Third Party:** This common exit strategy involves selling the business to an outside buyer. This could be a competitor, a larger company seeking to expand its footprint, or a financial investor. You might achieve this through a direct sale with a lump sum settlement or contracted payments. A broker could also help to accomplish it.

- **Pass to Family or Employees:** You might want to consider transferring ownership to family members or employees to keep the business in familiar hands. If you plan to keep the business in the family, you need to identify the successor early and gradually involve them in business operations to ensure a smooth transition. You'll also want to provide formal education or hands-on training in every aspect of the business.

- **Public Offering:** Going public is a significant exit strategy for larger companies. It involves selling a portion of the business to public investors. This requires adhering to regulatory standards, achieving transparency in operations, and, often, a reorganization of the business structure.

- **Private Offering:** Selling shares to private investors or private equity firms can be an alternative to an IPO. This might be suitable for business owners who want their investment to grow before a complete exit or wish to sell a stake without public reporting requirements.

- **Merger or Acquisition:** Combining with another business or having your company acquired by a larger firm can provide an exit strategy that also strengthens your business's market position or operational capabilities. Competitors and companies in complementary industries are often interested in this kind of transaction.

- **Liquidation:** If no suitable buyers are found or if the business cannot be sustained, liquidation might be necessary. This means selling all assets and closing the business.

The value of your business will be different in each scenario. Before you enter the agreement, you'll need to know which valuation method will be used—earnings multiples, discounted cash flows, or asset-based valuation. Market conditions can also significantly affect the success of your exit strategy. For instance, an IPO might not be advisable during a market downturn, whereas a direct sale could still be viable. The timing of your exit can affect both the financial outcome and the ease of transition. Consider both market and personal timing when planning your exit. Additionally, some exits, like IPOs or passing to a family member, require years of preparation, while others, such as a direct sale, can be executed more quickly if the business is already in good shape.

Preparing for a healthy exit means enhancing the value of your business to maximize profit.

No matter which exit strategy you choose, preparing for a healthy exit means enhancing the value of your business to maximize profit. The strategies we mentioned earlier to help grow your business will prove useful as you implement your exit strategy. Managing debt, optimizing cash flow, and keeping comprehensive, transparent records will ensure you have robust financials when you make the move.

More importantly, entrepreneurs must streamline operations to ensure the business can run efficiently without their daily involvement. A strong management team that can operate the business without you will facilitate this step. A business independent from the owner is important to potential buyers and helps achieve a smoother transition.

You can also expedite the exit process by making sure all legal aspects, such as intellectual property rights, contracts, and corporate structure, are in order.

Like your business plan, your exit strategy will need regular reviews and revisions. As personal circumstances or markets change, what might have seemed like the best exit strategy when you started might be different two years later. The advisory network you created to get your business started can help update your exit strategy as needed. Their professional insights can ensure that your strategy remains relevant and effective.

Key Takeaways

- **A successful business is an evolving and growing organism.** This means entrepreneurs must constantly look for ways to improve products, services, and operational processes and remain responsive to customer feedback and market trends.

- **Retaining an existing customer is generally more cost-effective than acquiring a new one.**

- **Performance monitoring is essential.** It allows you to gauge your business's health and understand how well it is achieving its objectives.

- **Invest in your team** by providing educational opportunities and training.

- **Scaling your business** increases revenue and makes it more attractive to buyers when you are ready to exit.

12

Leaving a Family Legacy

Building a business that endures beyond a single lifetime creates a lasting impact, cements a family's financial security, and establishes a generational legacy. This requires a strong foundational system, a clear vision, and a culture that aligns with the long-term growth and sustainability in your business.

A stable entity that serves the current market and is robust enough to support and enrich future generations requires meticulous planning, a deep understanding of the business landscape, and a commitment to foundational values that foster long-term success.

Establish a Strong Foundational Systems

Strong foundational business models are adaptable yet resilient to market changes. Much of what we've discussed in terms of diversifying revenue streams, optimizing cost structures, exploring new market opportunities, and creating scalable operations applies to legacy businesses. One of the most overlooked areas in the family business is the need to cultivate a leadership approach that focuses on long-term objectives rather than short-term gains.

Encourage active participation from all family members, regardless of their current role in the business. Everyone should feel that their contributions are welcomed and valued. They need to understand the mission and values of the company and maintain a commitment to uphold them. This means the founder must clearly define and regularly reaffirm the company's mission and core values. These should resonate with all aspects of the business operations and help steer the company through evolving markets and internal changes.

Successors should also be engaged in continuous planning processes, helping to revise and adapt strategies as the business and external environments evolve. This includes forecasting industry trends and preparing the business for upcoming challenges and opportunities. The mission and values should also include a commitment to sustainable practices that protect the environment and contribute positively to society. This ensures the business's compliance with increasing regulatory demands and builds a positive brand image that attracts modern consumers and employees.

Involving Family in Business

By introducing family members to your endeavor early, you provide them with opportunities to learn and grow within the company. This strategic approach can significantly contribute to the seamless transition of leadership and operations across generations.

Young family members can be exposed to the company in a variety of ways. Informal discussions at home or allowing them to join you at work occasionally are excellent ways to involve your children or heirs. Let them help with business-related tasks suitable to their age and interest levels often. Plus, there can be significant tax benefits to hiring young family members. See Chapter 9 of Tax-Free Wealth© for more details.

As family members grow, internships and part-time positions within the company can be invaluable. The roles they take on should genuinely contribute to the business, while helping them understand the workings of the company and the industry. Allow them to explore every part of the business applicable to their age and interest. This early exposure lets them understand the company's processes, challenges, and market environment from the ground up and can foster a deep understanding of the business's core operations and strategic positioning.

Early involvement also helps them develop necessary business skills in a real-world context.

Early involvement also helps them develop necessary business skills in a real-world context. Learning on the job allows them to apply theoretical knowledge in practical situations, enhancing their learning curve. It also prepares them for future leadership roles and allows them to get a feel for which positions might be most attractive to them later in life.

When young people reach college age, encourage formal education or other hands-on learning. Whether it's business management, finance, marketing, or other relevant discipline, having a solid educational foundation will equip them with the knowledge needed to contribute effectively to the business. Leadership training and working alongside leaders will also help prepare them to take on higher responsibilities when the time comes.

Being involved in the business early creates a sense of commitment and loyalty to the family legacy. This emotional investment often translates into a stronger dedication to the business's success and continuity.

At the same time, be sure to balance family involvement with meritocracy. Family members should earn their positions based on capability and performance, just like other employees, and their roles should be clearly defined. This approach ensures that the business maintains high standards and that family members are respected by other team members.

Assess the interest and willingness of family members to be involved in the business. Forcing involvement can lead to disinterest or worse, so their participation must be driven by genuine interest.

By implementing thoughtful strategies that encourage early learning, practical involvement, and leadership preparation, you can create a robust foundation for a successful generational transition.

If you've developed a culture of continuous learning within your organization, it will be easy to pass this value along to family members who may one day take over. Continuous learning helps family members stay updated with industry trends and business practices.

Nothing advances learning faster than hands-on experience. Implementing rotational assignments where family members work in different departments or branches of the business provides an invaluable experience. It gives your heirs a comprehensive understanding of how the business operates from various perspectives.

You might also consider pairing family members with experienced mentors within the business. Young adults will come to value those they might look down on otherwise. Plus, these mentors can guide them, provide feedback, and help them navigate their career paths within the company.

As family members grow in their roles, assign them to lead projects. This responsibility helps build their confidence and skills in managing teams and making decisions under supervision initially and with greater autonomy over time.

Encourage family members to gain experience outside the family business. Working in different companies, especially in similar industries, can provide new insights and experiences that they can bring back to the family business. Along those same lines, support their participation in industry conferences, trade shows, and other networking events. These platforms offer valuable learning experiences and the opportunity to meet other professionals and leaders, broadening their perspective and professional network.

Encourage family members to gain experience outside the family business.

Those who will one day take over the company should be subject to regular performance reviews to assess their progress and areas for improvement. These reviews should be as rigorous as those for other employees to maintain professionalism and objectivity. They also establish a robust feedback mechanism that allows family members to understand their strengths and areas where they need to improve. Constructive feedback is crucial for continuous personal and professional development.

Ensuring that family members have clearly defined roles and responsibilities is crucial for the smooth operation and professional management of a family business. It helps prevent conflicts, increases operational efficiency, and ensures that each person's contributions are valuable and aligned with the business's objectives.

As you did for yourself when you embarked on the entrepreneurial journey, assess the skills, education, and professional interests of each family member involved in the business and analyze the company's needs. Understanding strengths and weaknesses as well as present and future roles needed allows younger family members to fill positions they are well-suited to and passionate about.

Create formal job descriptions with specific responsibilities, expectations, and the metrics used to evaluate their performance. Making sure job descriptions meet professional standards comparable to those of similar roles in the industry helps maintain professionalism within the business and sets clear expectations for family members.

The clear communication channels you set up for your employees will prove essential for family members migrating into the business. Effective communication is a skill that can be learned and improves the overall dialogue regarding succession planning. Regular family meetings dedicated to succession planning and formal presentations that clearly outline the plan can help clarify complex information. Not only will these systems provide additional feedback loops and improve operations, but they will also allow you to maintain healthy family relationships.

Effective communication is a skill that can be learned and improves the overall dialogue regarding succession planning.

In the same way, conflict resolution mechanisms are vital. Have a plan in place to address conflicts that may arise from overlapping responsibilities or personal disagreements. Cultivate an environment where differing opinions are respected and considered. This formal process will help resolve issues professionally and fairly, and the respect it fosters will create an atmosphere conducive to open and honest communication. In some cases, external facilitators or mediators can help manage communication more effectively, especially when dealing with sensitive issues or conflicts within the family. These professionals can ensure that discussions remain constructive and that all voices are heard.

Succession Planning

A well-thought-out succession plan secures the continuity of the business while also respecting the legacy of the founders and preparing future leaders. Creating a structured and detailed succession plan is crucial to ensure smooth transitions of leadership and management responsibilities.

To avoid miscommunication and hard feelings, identify potential successors early in the process. Look for individuals who possess the necessary skills and disposition and have a deep commitment to the values and vision of the business. Defining a clear timeline for the transition process will be exceedingly valuable. Include significant milestones leading up to the full transfer of responsibilities as well as the roles and responsibilities of the successor. This schedule will give a detailed picture of the phasing out of one generation and the phasing in of the next.

Work with legal and accounting professionals to address the transfer of ownership shares, revision of business structure, and any contracts or agreements related to the succession. A clear financial plan should also be part of the succession process, addressing issues such as estate planning, tax implications of transferring business ownership, and financial security for the outgoing generation. Your succession plan should undergo regular reviews and updates to reflect any changes in the business environment, family circumstances, or potential successors' readiness and suitability.

A successful succession plan often includes a mentorship program with clear objectives. At the outset, mentors should know the specific skills and knowledge mentees need, the professional qualities they should develop, and the understanding of the business culture they should gain. Pairing current leaders with future successors ensures a transfer of knowledge and company values and ensures that the leadership transition is smooth and effective.

Choose mentors based on their expertise, leadership qualities, and commitment to the company's values. These individuals will provide and recommend training on the critical aspects of business and leadership. Ideal mentors are experienced leaders with a deep understanding of the business and are skilled communicators.

Carefully pair mentors with successors based on compatibility, career interests, and developmental needs. The right match can enhance the learning experience, ensuring that mentees receive guidance tailored to their specific needs and aspirations.

Ensure that both mentors and mentees have the necessary resources to succeed. This includes setting aside time specifically for mentorship activities and shadowing, access to necessary financial and material resources, and administrative support. During this season, all relevant information about the business's performance, challenges, and strategic direction should be made available. This transparency helps build trust and prepares all involved for future responsibilities.

Remember that family mentorship can sometimes be emotionally and professionally challenging. Provide support mechanisms, such as access to external coaching or counseling, to help participants navigate these challenges.

Mentorship is a strategic investment to help successors be better prepared to take on leadership roles. If you've created a culture that values learning and development, your entire team will respect the mentorship relationships and recognize the contributions of both mentors and mentees. They'll understand that future leaders will be equipped with practical experience, a clear grasp of their responsibilities, and a strong alignment with the business's core values.

Look for unique educational opportunities for family members entering the business. In addition to the variety of learning means we mentioned earlier, consider financial simulations or case studies specific to your industry or business model to help family members apply financial concepts in a controlled, risk-free environment. Offer incentives for completing financial education courses or achieving certain milestones in personal financial management. Incentives could include recognition, rewards, or even greater involvement in major financial decision-making processes.

You can also leverage technology and digital tools to maintain continuous communication, especially if family members are not always physically present. Tools like family business intranets, secure messaging apps, and regular newsletters can keep everyone updated and engaged.

Creating Generational Wealth

Even before you feel the freedom available in entrepreneurship, understand the pivotal role it can play in generational wealth creation. You can build a legacy that offers you and your family a unique pathway to financial independence and security or allows you to engage in philanthropy and community involvement.

Unlike traditional employment, entrepreneurship often allows for significant capital accumulation through a variety of means. Successful entrepreneurs can transform their innovative ideas and business operations into valuable assets that appreciate over time, leading to wealth and equity accumulation. As the business grows and becomes more profitable, its value increases, turning into a significant source of wealth for the entrepreneur and their family, potentially offering long-term financial security.

Entrepreneurship provides the flexibility to diversify income sources. Beyond the primary business operations, entrepreneurs can expand into related areas, invest in other businesses, or establish passive income streams, such as rental properties or stocks and bonds. Each type of asset offers different levels of risk and return but allows the entrepreneur to mitigate risk by spreading out potential losses and enhancing financial security. The choice of investment depends on the entrepreneur's financial goals, risk tolerance, and market conditions.

Entrepreneurship provides the flexibility to diversify income sources.

Real estate can be an excellent source of passive income through rental properties or a substantial capital gain through property appreciation. Entrepreneurs can use profits from the business to invest in commercial properties, residential rentals, or other real estate investments.

Investing in stocks, bonds, and mutual funds offers opportunities for wealth growth through dividends, interest income, and capital gains. Entrepreneurs should balance their portfolios across different sectors and risk levels to optimize their returns.

Starting side businesses related to the primary business can capitalize on existing expertise while exploring new markets.

You'll also want to weigh the implications of how your personal investments interact with your business finances. In some cases, you may want to invest directly through your business for tax or strategic reasons.

Before investing, thoroughly assess the risks associated with different types of assets. Consider factors such as market volatility, economic trends, and potential returns. This assessment will help you make informed decisions that align with your overall financial strategy. You'll also want to ensure some investments are easily liquidated, providing quick access to cash if needed. Liquidity is crucial for managing unforeseen expenses or taking advantage of new investment opportunities. Additionally, some investments have unforeseen legal and tax implications. Consult with financial advisors and tax professionals to navigate these complexities and optimize the tax benefits associated with various investments.

One of the most significant aspects of entrepreneurship in terms of family wealth is the ability to pass down assets across generations. This generational transfer can provide stability and financial security for the entrepreneur's descendants, giving them a solid foundation upon which to build.

The wealth generated from entrepreneurial ventures can fund educational opportunities for your family members. Your children and grandchildren can acquire higher education without the burden of debt. Additionally, it can provide seed capital for family members to start their own businesses, fostering a culture of entrepreneurship within the family.

Strategic business planning can lead to significant tax benefits, giving you additional wealth creation and preservation funds. Properly structured, a business can leverage various tax incentives, deductions, and credits to maximize financial outcomes.

Entrepreneurs who incorporate every strategic opportunity reinvest profits to fuel business growth. While this requires balancing personal financial needs with business development, strategic reinvestment can exponentially increase the business's value.

The exit strategy you choose will also become a crucial means of generational wealth. Whether it's a sale, merger, or public offering, a well-planned exit can maximize the financial returns from an entrepreneurial venture.

Preserve the Business Legacy

By carefully planning the distribution and management of personal and business assets, families can safeguard assets from potential risks, including business liabilities, lawsuits, and creditors. Proper planning ensures that valuable assets are structured in a way that protects the legacy and allows it to be passed on efficiently to future generations.

One primary goal of estate planning is to facilitate a smooth transition of assets and responsibilities from one generation to the next. This includes clear instructions on asset distribution, helping to prevent family disputes, and ensuring that the business continues operating with minimal disruption.

Given the complexities of estate laws and tax regulations, working with experienced estate planning attorneys, financial advisors, and tax professionals specializing in family businesses is advisable. These experts can provide tailored advice based on the family's specific circumstances and business structure.

As your business and personal financial states change and grow, your estate plan needs to be reviewed and modified. An estate plan is not static; regular reviews ensure your plans remain effective and relevant, adapting to new family members, business growth, or legal changes.

Involve family members in the estate planning process to educate them about the purposes and structures of the plan. This involvement helps in smooth implementation and prepares future generations to manage their inheritance responsibly.

A will is foundational and the most common element in estate planning. This document details how personal and business assets should be distributed upon the owner's death. It also names executors who will manage the estate's affairs.

Often, when an individual puts a will in place, they will also ask their lawyer to draw up other estate planning documents, such as a family trust. For families who own businesses, buy-sell agreements are essential. These outline what happens to a business owner's share of the company if they die, become incapacitated, or choose to leave the business. These agreements help ensure the business remains within the family or is sold under agreed-upon terms, preventing potential external takeover or internal conflict.

For families who own businesses, buy-sell agreements are essential.

Powers of attorney are another legal document for entrepreneurs who recognize the need to have a plan in place in the event they become temporarily unable to make decisions. This grants someone the authority to handle financial or legal matters on behalf of the estate owner if they become incapacitated so the business can continue to operate.

Many estate plans include a healthcare directive as part of their estate planning. Like a power of attorney, a healthcare directive specifies an individual's preferences for medical care if they are unable to make decisions themselves and designates a representative to make healthcare decisions on their behalf.

In addition to a will, trusts can give clear directions on the management and distribution of assets over time. The founder can specify how and when beneficiaries receive assets, preventing misuse of wealth or spending irresponsibly. They can also help the owner's heirs avoid the legal challenges of probating their will.

Trusts can be particularly useful in setting aside assets for specific purposes, such as funding future education or supporting philanthropic endeavors. Trusts also provide greater control over the timing and conditions under which assets are distributed. With proper planning with a strong tax advisor, trusts can even mitigate current and future income, gift, and estate taxes.

A trust can hold ownership or shares of a family business, including an FLP, LLC, or S corporation, ensuring that the business does not have to be sold or divided upon the death of the founder. This helps maintain business continuity and stability, as operational control can be seamlessly transferred according to predetermined rules set out in the trust agreement.

Four Types of Trusts Used by Family Business

- **Revocable Trusts**: Also known as living trusts or family trusts, these are created during the lifetime of the founder and can be altered or revoked as circumstances change. This flexibility makes them ideal for family businesses as it allows the founder to retain control over the assets while alive and ensure they are transferred smoothly after their death.

- **Irrevocable Trusts**: Once established, these trusts cannot be easily altered or revoked. They offer greater protection from creditors and can be advantageous for tax reasons, as the transferred assets are generally removed from the founder's taxable estate.

- **Dynasty Trusts**: These are designed to last for multiple generations and can protect the family wealth from estate taxes over an extended period, far beyond the founder's lifetime. They are a powerful tool for ensuring long-term financial security and maintaining control over the distribution of assets across generations.

- **Charitable Remainder Trusts**: Charitable Remainder Trusts allow the founder to receive income from the trust for a set period, with the remainder going to a designated charity. This type of trust can be beneficial for tax planning and supporting philanthropic goals.

If you're considering setting up a trust for your business or personal assets, first clearly define what you aim to achieve and which trust structure best meets the needs of your goals, including tax implications. Whether protecting assets, providing for the family, ensuring business continuity, or continuing to give to charities after you've gone, understanding these goals will guide the type of trust and the terms set within it.

Establishing a trust involves complex legal and financial considerations. Work with estate planning attorneys, tax advisors and financial advisors with family business experience to ensure that the trust is set up correctly and effectively. As with all aspects of estate planning, openly communicate with family members about the purposes and mechanics of the trust. This transparency helps prevent misunderstandings and conflicts later on.

Trusts can also protect assets from creditors, lawsuits, and other claims, which is particularly important for preserving the business's assets for future generations. Certain types of trusts can shield assets from the personal liabilities of the beneficiaries.

Choosing the right legal structure is critical for preserving the family business. It can impact everything from tax liability and operational flexibility to succession planning and the ease of transfer of ownership. Certain structures offer specific benefits that can be particularly advantageous for family-owned enterprises, such as minimizing taxes and streamlining the transition of ownership across generations. We looked at some of these options earlier, but when you consider legacy planning, they offer another set of benefits.

A Family Limited Partnership (FLP) is a unique type of limited partnership specifically geared toward legacy businesses because family members hold all the shares. In this partnership, one or more general partners manage the business, and other members are limited partners who are typically passive investors.

FLPs can provide a layer of protection from creditors, as the personal assets of the limited partners are protected from the partnership's liabilities. Plus, they may offer tax benefits, such as the ability to gift shares of the partnership to other family members at reduced tax rates, thus facilitating the gradual transfer of wealth and reducing estate taxes. Finally, general partners retain control over the management of the

FLP, allowing senior family members to manage the business while gradually transferring wealth to the next generation.

We discussed the S Corporation earlier, and you might remember that these pass-through entities allow income to be taxed only at the shareholder level, not at the corporate level, potentially reducing the total tax burden. One great advantage for the family business is that shares of an S corporation can be transferred to family members without triggering income tax, facilitating smooth succession planning. The limited liability aspect of S corporations protects the shareholder's personal assets from the corporation's liabilities, providing financial security for family members. Keep in mind that transferring any assets, including ownership in an S corporation, can have gift tax consequences.

Limited Liability Companies allow for a flexible management structure. This can be particularly advantageous for family businesses that may want to tailor governance according to their specific needs. LLCs can be taxed as pass-through entities (partnership or S corporation) and can also be structured to allow for easy transfer of ownership without complex legal hurdles, which is ideal for succession planning.

Role of Legal and Financial Advisors in Family Business Planning

In the complex landscape of family business management and estate planning, the guidance of the network of legal and financial advisors you built is invaluable. If legacy building is part of your business goal, you'll want to make sure your legal and financial network can address the specific needs of family businesses and estate planning. This expertise includes tax planning, business law, estate and trust law, and financial management for families. Their familiarity with common issues and strategies in these areas can provide more tailored and effective advice.

Advisors provide an objective perspective essential for making informed decisions, especially in emotionally charged situations like family business planning. This objectivity helps ensure decisions are made based on sound business practices and legal principles. They can also help identify and manage potential risks associated with business operations and wealth transfer. This can include legal liabilities, tax implications, and financial exposures for your family that might not be apparent to those without professional expertise.

Advisors can help you choose the right business structure for your family and provide guidance to minimize tax liabilities. This can involve strategic allocation of investments, timing of income, and utilization of tax-advantaged savings accounts.

In addition to drafting wills, trusts, and other estate documents that ensure assets are protected and passed on according to the owner's wishes, legal advisors can help navigate complex family dynamics and ensure all legal requirements are met to avoid future disputes.

Your network of advisors also plays a role in crafting plans for the smooth transition of leadership and ownership in the family business. They can assist you in developing training programs for successors, setting up governance structures, and planning for continuity. Whenever possible, involve both legal and financial advisors in planning sessions. Their combined insights can lead to more holistic strategies that cover all bases, from legal protections to financial optimizations.

Keep Your Legacy Up-to-Date

The dynamic nature of personal relationships, business conditions, and legal frameworks in a family business necessitates the regular updating of legal documents such as wills, trusts, and succession plans. As a family business grows or diversifies, changes might occur in its structure, valuation, or operations. These changes can have significant implications for how assets are handled in estate plans or succession strategies. Marriages, births, divorces, or deaths also alter the relationships and roles within the family. Your advisors may need to make adjustments to how assets are distributed, or roles are defined in business succession plans.

As with non-family businesses, laws governing estates, trusts, and businesses can change, and tax regulations have the potential to shift. Keeping documents updated in line with these changes is crucial to avoid unintended consequences or inefficiencies.

As family members reach certain milestones, such as coming of age, graduation, or retirement, their roles and stakes in the family business may need reevaluation. **Review estate documents at least every three to five years.** Such milestones often prompt a review of existing plans to ensure they still align with the individual's and the business's current needs and goals.

Be sure to review these aspects of your business during each of your regular reviews. Review estate documents at least every three to five years or after any significant change in personal or business circumstances. Keep a log of any changes made to legal documents, including the reasons for these changes. This record can be invaluable for future planning and legal clarity should disputes arise.

When updating any document, you'll want to consider its implications on other related documents. For example, changes to a will might affect the relevance or effectiveness of related trusts or buy-sell agreements within the business. Ensure consistency across all legal documents to avoid conflicts or ambiguities. Designations on retirement accounts and insurance policies should align with the wishes expressed in a will or trust. Communicate any changes in legal documents clearly to all relevant parties, including family members, business partners, and key employees. This clarity prevents misunderstandings and ensures smooth implementation of the updated plans.

Key Takeaways

- **Include potential successors from a very young age.** Phase family members into the business as early as possible.

- **Use mentors to effectively train and prepare future leaders.**

- **Consider the possibility of a trust to help protect your assets for generations.** There are a variety of ways your business can be part of a trust that will help your business provide funds for future generations.

- **Consult professionals with experience in legacy businesses.**

Acknowledgments

From Beau: Writing this book has been an incredible journey, and I am grateful for the many people who have supported me along the way.

First, I would like to thank my family for their endless encouragement and patience. To my wife, Briceida, your unwavering belief in me has been my greatest motivation. Thank you for being my rock through every late night and early morning. To my son, Baby Beau, your smiles and love keep me grounded and remind me of the legacy I hope to build.

To my mom, for spending countless hours with me on my entrepreneurial journey and giving me the support only a mother could. Your love, wisdom, and belief in me have been a constant source of strength, and I am forever grateful for everything you have done.

I am also deeply thankful to my co-author, Tom, for your partnership in this project. Your insights and expertise in business ownership and tax strategy have pushed me to grow in ways I never imagined. It has been a privilege to collaborate with someone whose work I have long admired. Many of your books have a permanent place on my bookshelf, and they've been instrumental in shaping my knowledge and passion for these subjects.

To Bill Davis, my "Marketing MacGyver," thank you for your guidance and ingenuity over the past dozen-plus years. You have been instrumental in my growth, and I am lucky to have had your support and creative solutions through every challenge.

To my business partners, mentors, and colleagues, your constant support and wisdom have shaped not only this book but also my personal and professional growth. Thank you for your generosity in sharing your knowledge and experience.

Lastly, to my readers—this book is for you. I hope it brings you the inspiration and tools to pursue your dreams. Thank you for allowing me to be a part of your journey.

—Beau Eckstein

From Tom: I appreciate Beau asking me to become involved in this book about the transition from employee to entrepreneur. I began my transition in 1995 without any of this guidance. I often think about how much guidance like this book, or the opportunity to own a franchise instead of starting my business from scratch, might have reduced the stress of leaving Corporate America and joining the ranks of the entrepreneur.

I would also like to express my gratitude to my partners and mentors along the way. My business partner of 24 years, Ann Mathis, took so much off my plate and I am eternally grateful for her guidance and unwavering belief in our business. Her passing has left a hole in my life and our business that cannot be filled.

My association with my friend and mentor, Robert Kiyosaki, has been invaluable. His teachings have helped millions around the world enjoy the benefits of entrepreneurship.

Never has there been anyone more passionate about creating and serving entrepreneurs as my friend Robert. He has taught me how to better teach entrepreneurs and the meaning of being a mission-driven entrepreneur. I am also grateful to him for writing the foreword to each of my books, including this one, and including me in several of his own books.

The love of my life is my wife, Louanne. She keeps me focused and always provides the best counsel and advice when I most need them.

Thanks most of all to you, our readers, who are thinking about taking the bold step of engaging in this wonderful world we call entrepreneurship. To you, I would say, don't hesitate. There is amazing joy and satisfaction in moving from Paycheck to Power.

—Tom Wheelwright

About the Authors

Tom Wheelwright®, CPA, is a tax and wealth expert and a serial entrepreneur dedicated to the belief that everyone deserves to be financially independent of employers, Wall Street, and the government. His businesses — WealthAbility®, TFW Advisors®, PLA Software, and Wheelwright Manahan Family Office — provide the education, tax preparation, tools, and teams that enable people to experience that freedom.

Wheelwright is a Rich Dad Advisor, the CPA for Robert Kiyosaki, an international speaker, and the author of the best-selling books The Win-Win Wealth Strategy and Tax-Free Wealth. He has spoken on stage on six continents to over 100,000 entrepreneurs, small business owners, and investors. He also hosts the popular podcast The WealthAbility® Show with Tom Wheelwright® CPA.

CONNECT WITH TOM

Follow him on Instagram & YouTube today.

TFWAdvisors.us

Beau Eckstein resides in Henderson, Nevada, where he leverages his extensive experience as a business ownership coach, broker, SBA loan advisor, and real estate investor. Beau owns several business ventures and helps entrepreneurs secure funding to grow their businesses.

Passionate about empowering business owners, Beau organizes the 'Business Ownership Summit,' providing valuable insights into business acquisition, franchise investments, SBA financing, and creative finance.

He assists clients in finding their ideal business, working with a diverse range of people from blue-collar workers starting their first business to serial entrepreneurs.

Married to Briceida and a proud father of a brand new baby boy, Beau is dedicated to supporting others in their entrepreneurial journeys while nurturing his own growing family.

Beau's goal is to help 10,000 aspiring entrepreneurs start their own businesses in the next 10 years.

CONNECT WITH BEAU

Follow him on your favorite
social media platforms today.

LinqApp.com/Beau_Eckstein

ARE YOU READY TO EXPERIENCE THE WORLD'S FIRST STRATEGIC TAX ADVISORY FRANCHISE?

TFW Advisors

Everyone deserves to be financially independent of employers, Wall Street and the government. TFW Advisors™ is dedicated to providing access to the tools, tax preparation, education, and teams that will empower people worldwide to create their own financial independence.

TFWAdvisors.us

THIS BOOK IS PROTECTED INTELLECTUAL PROPERTY

Instant IP ™

The author of this book values Intellectual Property and has utilized Instant IP, a groundbreaking technology.
Instant IP is the patented, blockchain-based solution for Intellectual Property protection.

Blockchain is a distributed public digital record that can not be edited. Instant IP timestamps the author's ideas, creating a smart contract, thus an immutable digital asset that proves ownership and establishes a first to use / first to file event.

Protected by Instant IP ™

LEARN MORE AT INSTANTIP.TODAY